ORTHO® ALL ABOUT BUILDING

Waterfalls,
Ponds, and Streams

Meredith® Books
Des Moines, Iowa

All About Building Waterfalls, Ponds, and Streams
Editor: Denny Schrock
Project Editor: Elsa Kramer
Contributing Editor: Kate Carter Frederick
Contributing Technical Editor: Michael D. Smith
Contributing Writer: Amy McDowell
Copy Chief: Terri Fredrickson
Publishing Operations Manager: Karen Schirm
Senior Editor, Asset and Information Manager:
    Phillip Morgan
Edit and Design Production Coordinator: Mary Lee Gavin
Editorial Assistant: Kathleen Stevens
Book Production Managers: Pam Kvitne,
    Marjorie J. Schenkelberg, Rick von Holdt, Mark Weaver
Photographers: Scott Little, Blaine Moats, Jay Wilde
Contributing Copy Editor: Lorraine Ferrell
Technical Proofreader: Richard Koogle
Contributing Proofreaders: Juliet Jacobs, Stephanie Petersen,
    Barbara Rothfus
Contributing Designer: Jeff Harrison
Contributing Map Illustrator: Jana Fothergill
Contributing Photo Researcher: Susan Ferguson
Indexer: Ellen Sherron
Other Contributors: Adams Aquatics, Aquascape Designs, Inc.,
    Beckett Water Gardening, Liquid Landscape Designers

**Additional Editorial Contributions from
  Art Rep Services**
Director: Chip Nadeau
Designer: lk Design

Meredith® Books
Executive Director, Editorial: Gregory H. Kayko
Executive Director, Design: Matt Strelecki
Managing Editor: Amy Tincher-Durik
Executive Editor/Group Manager: Benjamin W. Allen
Senior Associate Design Director: Tom Wegner
Marketing Product Manager: Brent Wiersma

Publisher and Editor in Chief: James D. Blume
Editorial Director: Linda Raglan Cunningham
Executive Director, New Business Development:
    Todd M. Davis
Executive Director, Sales: Ken Zagor
Director, Operations: George A. Susral
Director, Production: Douglas M. Johnston
Director, Marketing: Amy Nichols
Business Director: Jim Leonard

Vice President and General Manager: Douglas J. Guendel

Meredith Publishing Group
President: Jack Griffin
Executive Vice President: Bob Mate

Meredith Corporation
Chairman and Chief Executive Officer: William T. Kerr
President and Chief Operating Officer: Stephen M. Lacy

In Memoriam: E.T. Meredith III (1933–2003)

Contributing Photographers:
(Photographers credited may retain copyright © to the listed
    photographs.)
L = Left, R = Right, B = Bottom, T = Top

Liz Ball/Positive Images: 18T; **Gay Bumgarner:** 26T, 27T;
Gay Bumgarner/Positive Images: 20TL; **Rob Cardillo:** 79,
114; **R. Todd Davis:** 23B; **Catriona Tudor Erler:** 1, 100T;
Robert Fenner: 37; **Garden World Images:** 91; **Harry
Haralambou/Positive Images:** 55BR; **Jerry Harpur:** 24
(David Hicks); **Marcus Harpur:** 57T (Jinny Blom);
Doug Hetherington: 38T, 54T, 66, 70; **Jerry Howard/
Positive Images:** 17T; **Bill Johnson:** 27B; **Dency Kane:** 11B;
Rosemary Kautzky: 83T, 86, 88, 89, 93, 94, 95, 99R;
Janet Loughrey: 7T, 19B (Eamonn Hughes), 20TR;
Clive Nichols: 55BL, 77; **Jerry Pavia:** 8, 12, 13T, 29T, 97,
106T; **Alec Scaresbrook/Garden Picture Library:** 40B;
Ron Sutherland/Garden Picture Library: 18B; **Peter
Symcox/gardenimage:** 28B (Robin Hopper); **Michael
Thompson:** 4, 6, 7B, 13B, 15T, 20B, 21, 23T, 29B, 32, 36,
87T, 105B; **Justyn Willsmore:** 55T; **Gary G. Wittstock/
Garden Picture Library:** 16

Cover photograph: Catriona Tudor Erler

All of us at Meredith® Books are dedicated to providing
you with the information and ideas you need to enhance
your home and garden. We welcome your comments and
suggestions about this book. Write to us at:
    Meredith Corporation
    Meredith Gardening Books
    1716 Locust St.
    Des Moines, IA 50309–3023

If you would like more information on other Ortho
products, call 800/225-2883 or visit us at: www.ortho.com

Copyright © 2006 The Scotts Miracle-Gro Company.
Second Edition.
Some text, photography, and artwork copyright © 2006
Meredith Corporation. All rights reserved. Printed in the
United States of America.
Library of Congress Control Number: 2005929498
ISBN: 0-89721-514-1

Note to the Readers: Due to differing conditions, tools, and
individual skills, Meredith Corporation assumes no
responsibility for any damages, injuries suffered, or losses
incurred as a result of following the information published
in this book. Before beginning any project, review the
instructions carefully, and if any doubts or questions
remain, consult local experts or authorities. Because codes
and regulations vary greatly, you always should check with
authorities to ensure that your project complies with all
applicable local codes and regulations. Always read and
observe all of the safety precautions provided by
manufacturers of any tools, equipment, or supplies,
and follow all accepted safety procedures.

Contents

WATER FEATURES IN YOUR GARDEN

Nothing brings more serenity to a garden than the gentle reflection of cool water in a pond. A meandering stream or cascading waterfall soothes and refreshes with subtle movement and music that draw people near. A water feature adds a focal point to your garden and provides a cool oasis in a hectic world, a place to retreat and relax. The natural sound of moving water can drown out noise from the busy world beyond.

Water features also delight gardeners and visitors with their ever-changing liveliness. Water is an essential component in a garden designed as a wildlife habitat. A waterfall or stream attracts everything from dragonflies and butterflies to songbirds and hummingbirds as well as amphibians and small mammals. You may hear a male toad crooning to attract a mate or see a sparrow hop carefully from a rock

▼ Take advantage of the natural attributes of your landscape with a pond or stream.

ledge into a shallow basin to bathe. Imagine being able to walk out into your yard, stroll over to your pond, and watch bright goldfish darting beneath the spreading leaves of jewel-toned water lilies. Eventually your fish may even swim over to greet you at feeding time.

Water gardens are surging in popularity as gardeners discover the joys of backyard ponds and streams. People with busy schedules enjoy water gardening because of the satisfying results possible with minimal maintenance. A well-designed and properly installed water garden can achieve its own balance and maintain itself with just a little routine care.

Building a water feature can be as easy or as complex as you want it to be. This book can help you select and analyze the site on which you want to build. Then it will lead you through the steps necessary to create a design that takes best advantage of your site. You will learn which materials and equipment you need for installing various types of waterfalls, ponds, and streams. A guide to maintenance, including seasonal tasks, will aid you in keeping your water feature in top working condition. You can also read specific, step-by-step instructions for a variety of projects designed to fit a wide range of water gardening designs. This book helps you focus on making the most natural-looking pond, stream, or waterfall. The pleasure and satisfaction will be all yours for years to come.

▲ Add a water feature to your garden to create a peaceful spot for reading, relaxing, and watching wildlife.

WATER GARDENS IN HISTORY

▲ Formal gardens have their roots in the ancient East, with symmetrical designs, tiled pools, and minimal plantings. Statuary and trees create a courtyard feel.

Water features have been used in gardens for thousands of years in many cultures throughout the world. Water gardening has its roots in the aqueducts and canals used in ancient civilizations to bring water from mountain springs and rivers into communities. Persians were the first to invent and use such technology more than 6,000 years ago.

A Persian garden was a walled courtyard constructed around a water basin. Narrow canals divided the courtyard into four beds. The Persian word *pairidaeza*, or "walled garden," has come to mean paradise. Walled garden courtyards were popular in many arid climates because the design offered protection from the hot desert sun and wind.

Similarly, ancient Egyptians routed floodwater from the Nile River to large basins. They created garden courtyards formally designed with rows of plants, fruit trees, and palm trees surrounding a rectangular pond stocked with fish and water lilies.

The Etruscans built the first public fountains in Italy. Spring water spouted from wall sculptures into semicircular catch basins. Gravity powered the fountains, so the water flowed continuously and was not recirculated.

Romans created lion-head and dolphin sculptures that spit water. They also designed large ornamental bowls with water bubbling up in the center, stairway fountains with water flowing over stone steps into a pool, and the first water jets to spray up into the air. Their fountains were also powered by gravity. Water flowed through a system of aqueducts from natural springs in the hills, sometimes more than 50 miles away.

Middle Eastern gardens during the Arab Empire were also enclosed in walled courtyards and formally designed. Large, brightly tiled basins held gently rippling fountains in the center. Water was so precious that these gardens included few plants. This design, sometimes referred to as Islamic garden style, spread through Egypt, North Africa, southern Spain, and India.

Early Oriental hill-and-pond garden design began in China and spread to Japan. The hills represent islands, and the pond symbolizes the sea. Vertical rocks and waterfalls suggested the mountains of southern China, while the Japanese combined low rock formations and plantings with still pools or gently trickling streams to evoke the topography of Japan. The hill-and-pond design developed as an art form over many centuries and came to be recognized throughout the world. It is widely used today to create natural-looking gardens even in urban settings.

Water gardens were popularized following the tremendous creativity of the Italian Renaissance. Designs were symmetrical and grandiose, including ornate statuary, lush plantings, and dramatic fountains bursting with movement and sound. Such style was repeated throughout Europe and Russia.

The Romantic Period's sweeping lawns, extensive plantings, and large informal ponds replaced the symmetrical garden design of the Renaissance. Two examples that exist today are New York City's Central Park, completed in 1878, and Monet's water garden at Giverny in France, built in the 1890s.

Interest in ornamental gardening came to the United States in the late 1800s. Wealthy Americans with large estates built huge native plantation gardens in the east and Persian *pairidaezas* in the sunny southwest. Landscape architects used water in the landscape to bring nature and recreation to the inhabitants of the country's rapidly developing cities. Gardeners used different

styles from all over the world to create uniquely American designs. By the 20th century, Americans had shifted from formal to abstract designs, creating asymmetrical and free-form gardens that were both functional and natural looking.

Over the centuries, water features have evolved in design and construction. The impetus for water movement has shifted from gravity, human effort, and steam pumps to solar power and electricity. Constraints of time, effort, and money are no longer an obstacle. Since flexible pond liners came on the market in the 1960s, homeowners have been able to afford the luxury of a water feature that they can build themselves. The popularity of home water gardens continues to inspire innovation in water feature construction, design, and equipment. A water garden is no longer just for the wealthy. Almost anyone can build one just about anywhere.

▲ **Many formal Western gardens are based on the Persian *pairidaeza* of more than 6,000 years ago, in which walled courtyards were constructed around simple pools.**

◀ **Centuries ago the Egyptians used catchbasins like this one to bring water into the garden.**

SITE SELECTION AND DESIGN

Water gardens are popular because they transform an ordinary garden into a delightful retreat. Choose from a wealth of possibilities, from a small, simple fishpond or a lotus bog to a multiple-tier waterfall or a cascading stream.

Artistic expression

Designing a water feature is a visionary project, whether you seek a creative outlet or a way to challenge your mechanical or building skills. Even if you don't view its design as an art form, a water feature becomes an artful addition to the landscape. Making a waterfall, a stream, a reflecting pool, or a koi pond also offers new gardening opportunities as you decide which aquatic and marginal plants to include and how to incorporate them.

▽ **Water features should complement the landscape, placed where they look most natural.**

Whatever your goals, completing the project—a permanent addition to your garden—will give you a sense of pride and accomplishment.

Home improvement

In addition, a well-designed landscape that includes a carefully constructed water feature could increase your property's resale value. Depending on the design, you can use a water feature to resolve a landscape problem, such as an uninteresting or sloping site, turning it into a decorative asset. Your design might help you build on top of soil that retains water or soil that won't support much plant life other than weeds. Following a trend toward more environmentally friendly landscapes, the newest aquascape technology and concepts in constructing water features imitate nature and give you ways to transform your property into a beautiful oasis.

▲ **A water garden offers a tranquil family gathering spot for relaxing or entertaining.**

CHOOSING A SITE

Water gardens are now within the budget and skill level of most homeowners. The tools and materials available today make water garden installation easier than ever. You can build a water feature in a large, expansive landscape or a small, urban backyard. Even so, for the water garden to be successful—and to get the most enjoyment from it—you must build it on the right site.

Before you decide on the final location, there are a number of things to keep in mind: your site conditions, including slope, soil, sun, shade, and wind; your intended use of the feature; climatic conditions in your region; access to utilities, and location of utility lines. Finding the perfect spot requires a balance among these elements.

Location, location, location

■ **Slope:** Check out your site. Consider the slope and grade of your yard and work with it. The lowest spot may look like the best place for a pond, but it's actually the worst. Rainwater flows into a low-lying pond, muddying the water, washing away your fish, and knocking over plants. Poor drainage can also cause runoff to well up underneath the pond liner, creating undesirable bubbles that rise to the surface and make your pond water look foul. Placing the pond just above the lowest spot avoids these problems.

▲ A small pond and waterfall tucked into a shady corner add depth, texture, and sound to an otherwise unused part of the yard.

▼ A natural slope on your property may be the perfect place for a stream and pool.

If your site slopes, you'll need to level it, either by grading it and building a retaining wall or by building up the downhill side of the pond by adding soil or rock. Compact the soil to prevent settling. Otherwise, water will run out of the pond and down the hill.

Fortunately, a sloped site has its benefits too. It's a perfect spot to add a waterfall. You can lay out a slope to include a stream that runs from an upper pond to a lower one. When building on a slope, make sure you have a clear, safe, and easy path on which to carry materials to the pond site.

■ **Soil:** Take into account the kind of soil you have. It can determine whether your installation will be easy or complicated. If the soil is especially hard and rocky, save yourself difficult digging and install an aboveground pond with either a flexible or preformed liner supported by a wood, stone, or masonry structure.

Sandy soil also comes with problems. It is difficult to work with when trying to install an in-ground pond formed from a flexible liner because the sand may cave in along the sides of the pond. Here, a preformed liner may be the answer. To use a flexible liner, you'll need to use cinder blocks or wooden timbers under the liner to shore up the sides and hold the edging.

Clay soil, although sometimes difficult to excavate, can be ideal for in-ground installations. Clay soil holds its shape, and flexible liners will conform to whatever configuration you dig.

■ **Sun, shade, wind:** Take an inventory of the sun and shade patterns in your yard to

determine whether your water garden location will give your plants the sunlight (or the shade) they require. Wind can also affect plant life. Strong winds speed evaporation from the pond and can break the stems of some tender plants or harm plants that thrive in tranquil water. If you must locate the pond in a wind-prone spot, erect a windscreen or plant shrubs for a windbreak.

▓ **Access:** Choose a location that's far enough away from potential obstacles that you'll have easy access to all sides of the pond. Existing landscape features such as fences, and utility sheds can affect easy access to the pond when you're performing maintenance chores. If there's a fence in the vicinity, put your water garden several feet away from it (local codes often specify a specific distance from a fence).

▓ **Utilities:** Call local utility companies before digging and ask them to locate the lines that run through your property. Most utilities will mark the locations without charge. Even if a utility line is deeper than your pond will be, don't put the pond over an existing line. Any future repairs on the line will tear up the pond.

Function

After site conditions, one of the most important aspects to consider when choosing a location is how you want to use the pond. Make sure that the function and view of your water feature are integral parts of the design, not afterthoughts. For example, you may want to connect a pond to a perennial bed, a patio, a deck, or other existing features. Study the configuration of the land and tuck your water feature into its contours. Here are some examples of your options.

Will you look out your family room window to see the waterfall? If so, place the waterfall to the back of the pond, facing the window. Add plantings behind it to frame the view.

If your plan for the water garden includes enjoying it while sitting on a deck, you'll want it close by, perhaps almost under the deck so it looks like water under a dock. Make sure that any waterfall you might include is installed high enough to be seen over the deck railing.

If your water garden will be the focal point of your landscape design, you'll want to situate it so you can take in the entire garden from one vantage point.

▲ **Choose a location that drains well and receives adequate sunlight for growing plants.**

If you want a water garden to fit in with your love of bird-watching, locate the bird feeders away from and downwind of the pond, to help reduce cleanup problems from hulls and spilled birdseed. A pond designed as a natural wildlife setting might fit better in a less-used part of the yard, connected to the rest of the landscape with a pebble or mulch path.

▲ **If your pond will be the focal point of your entire landscape design, locate it where you can see it from one or more rooms in your home.**

▲ **Edging and plantings that complement existing structures create a harmonious design.**

Design elements

Water gardens affect the perspective of your landscape and add an element of surprise. Placement of the pond in relation to the rest of your landscape is crucial. A water garden simply dropped in the middle of the yard looks adrift in a sea of green lawn. Adding a neat, symmetrical row of rocks around its edge just makes matters worse, creating an unnatural perimeter that accentuates the pond's lack of connection to its surroundings.

Think about how the location of a water feature can enhance your landscape. For example, a rectangular pond set with its length parallel to the main view from the house will make a yard seem longer. An informal design with the longer sides perpendicular to your line of sight will exaggerate the perspective and make the yard seem wider. Small pools are surprises in the landscape, adding interest for visitors who happen upon them. You can achieve this sense of delight by tucking a small pond into a side yard or around the bend of a curving flower bed. Add an arbored bench to complete your garden retreat.

Whatever you do, integrate the size, scale, and other elements of your water garden into the existing features of your landscape.

■ **Size:** Ponds, streams, and waterfalls can be installed in almost any size, shape, or configuration. Tuck one into a corner of your yard or build the pond so it looks as if it disappears underneath a deck.

Small yards can easily hold a water garden made from nothing more than a large pot or container set into the ground, either partially or completely beneath the soil line. A 2-foot-round hole, overlaid with a flexible liner and filled with moist soil, is ideal for a bog garden with a small lotus or a marginal water plant, such as iris or lizard's tail. It provides the perfect opportunity to add water plants to a perennial border when your yard is too small for a full-scale pond.

■ **Scale:** Scale is important when designing a water feature. A large waterfall can overpower a small landscape. A small pond in the midst of a large setting can look like a puddle.

There are some tricks that allow you to break the rules of scale. For example, if you would like to build a large pond on a small

◀ Keep your water feature in scale with the size of your yard. Leave room nearby for a place to sit and enjoy what you have created.

site, you can create islands, peninsulas, or decks that overhang the pond to break up the visual impact of the water so that it doesn't seem so large. Incorporating existing landscape as part of the overall water garden design can help give a small feature more impact.

Although there are no hard-and-fast rules about the relationship of pond size to yard size, you can estimate the effect of scale with a garden hose or colored twine. Lay out the hose or twine in the planned configuration of your pond, and then experiment until the scale seems right. Leave the trial outline in place for a week or so to help you decide if the placement of the pond will capitalize on the views from the house, patio, or other spots on your property. This trial run will also help you determine if the water feature fits with the natural traffic patterns in your landscape and whether it will leave enough room for outdoor furniture and decorative objects.

▦ **Edging:** Make sure to use an edging that complements other hardscape elements in your overall landscape design. Hardscape elements are those features in your yard that are constructed—decks, arbors, patios, walkways, and driveways, for example. If you've laid a certain type of rock on a path through your perennial bed, use that same rock to edge your water garden. Vary the size of the rocks around the pond so they look natural and visually appealing. Using similar materials in the pond and overall landscape help achieve a unified, harmonious garden design.

Using more than one kind of stone in the landscape can be challenging. For instance, if you use mixed fieldstone to edge the perennial bed and flagstone around the pond, either the fieldstone or the flagstone may look out of place. You don't always have to use the same stone,

though. A slate patio can be complemented with wood decking or a jagged stone of a similar color. Try to harmonize the separate elements without making one seem out of place or too dominant.

WATER FEATURES AND CHILD SAFETY

A water feature raises safety concerns, particularly when young children live near it. Plan ahead and provide for safety by following these suggestions:

▦ Never leave children unsupervised near water.

▦ If you have a toddler in your family, you might want to delay construction of the water feature. Meanwhile, make a large sandbox and convert it later into a pond or bog garden.

▦ As alternatives to a pond, consider building a fountain bubbling over stones or a dry creek that will carry water only during wet periods.

▦ Locate the feature within easy view of the house and the yard.

▦ Put a fence around your water feature or your property to keep neighborhood children from wandering onto the site. Your insurance coverage may require a tall fence with a childproof gate.

▦ Consider building a raised or partially raised pond that affords a measure of security.

▦ Cover the pond with a safety grate that rests securely a few inches below the water's surface but allows plants to grow through it. Add black or blue dye to the water to disguise the grate.

▦ For added safety, install a motion-sensitive alarm when you construct the feature.

▦ Ask local authorities about requirements for safety, permits, and inspection.

ANALYZING YOUR SITE

As you take a close, methodical look at your site to determine its physical characteristics and horticultural potential, you can assemble a needs list based on what your new water garden will allow. Whether your site is totally undeveloped or already well-established, careful analysis and planning can reveal its possibilities and limitations.

Draw a diagram

Working from a simple diagram will help you take accurate measurements and note the position of existing plantings and structures. Use letter-size architect's graph paper that is preprinted with squares in a ⅛-inch grid. If your site is larger than 30×40 feet, let each ⅛-inch square equal 1 foot; otherwise, let ¼ inch (2 squares) equal 1 foot. If possible, trace an existing scaled map included in your mortgage records, house plans, or property deed. Otherwise, ask someone to help you use a tape measure to plot the grid.

▲ **Situate your pond away from utility lines and easements and not directly under mature trees.**

Start by drawing in any structures within or adjacent to the site you have chosen for your water feature. Note buildings, driveways, patios, decks, walls, and fences. Mark the location of any windows and outer doors on existing buildings. While standing at each door and window, take note of the view. Is there natural scenery that will benefit from the addition of a water feature? Or do you see pavement or storage areas? Take note of unattractive views and think of ways to lessen their impact on your site's development. Include on your diagram any easements, setbacks, utility meters, underground and overhead power lines, downspouts, and drainage systems. Mark the location of any outdoor electrical outlets.

Next, indicate any mature trees and shrubs as well as existing garden beds. Label any areas with natural features such as rock outcrops. Unless your property is relatively flat, draw contour lines to indicate gradient changes. Let 1 contour line represent every 1-foot change in level. This will help you anticipate rainwater and runoff drainage patterns and map low spots where water collects. Keep in mind the potential problems of causing water to flow toward your house or someone else's property.

Check the soil and other natural elements

Now study the natural elements and the soil on your property. Record the following items on your diagram.

■ **Position and wind direction:** Use a compass to determine magnetic north and note it with an arrow on your diagram. Consult your local weather service or an almanac to determine the direction of prevailing winds in your area. Mark that on the diagram too. Check for areas on your site that may be especially exposed to wind.

■ **Special conditions:** Note areas that receive continuous sunlight and shady spots that receive little or no light. Keep in mind that sunny and shady spots change with the seasons, the angle of the sun, and the leafing and shedding of deciduous trees. Also note on your diagram any cold spots in low-lying areas or places where structures or plantings block air flow.

■ **Soil type:** Determine if the site you plan to dig is native soil, such as sand or clay, or if it contains construction debris or pockets of heavy or rocky soil. Indicate any areas on your diagram where excavation or planting may require extra effort.

Compare and create

Using the information you have marked on your diagram, make a list of your site's assets and problems, and keep the list handy for consultation. As you compare what you want to build with the potential of your site, a plan will begin to emerge. Experiment with designs on sheets of tracing paper laid over your base diagram. Draw circles to represent major areas or features. Use dashes and arrows to represent sight lines from viewpoint to object. Use larger arrows to indicate circulation patterns. How will people move from one point to another around your water feature? Is the path logical and safe? Does it offer the best views of the garden? This will be especially important if your site already has mature plantings. Your sketches may lead you to replace a straight brick path with a curving line of stepping-stones or to relocate some evergreens in order to accommodate new water-loving perennial flowers. Whatever your completed plan, a basic diagram of your site overlaid with some design ideas will help you to achieve your goals.

▲ Working from a simple diagram as you plan your water feature will help you achieve the finished look you want.

▶ Natural contours in the land will affect drainage patterns. Direct water away from low spots and also away from your neighbor's property.

A BALANCED ECOSYSTEM

The nitrogen cycle converts harmful chemical elements into harmless and beneficial elements. Fish waste and plant debris contain ammonia (NH_3), which is toxic to fish. Beneficial bacteria tackle the ammonia in two steps. Aerobic bacteria use oxygen to break down ammonia into nitrites (NO_2). Then anaerobic bacteria break down nitrites into nitrates (NO_3) without oxygen. The process releases nitrogen gas into the atmosphere, while plants take up the nitrates to fuel growth. (See pages 48–49 for more information on the nitrogen cycle.)

Algae are always present in a pond ecosystem. In a balanced pond the nitrogen cycle naturally keeps all elements, including the algae population, in check. At the design stage, you can take into consideration several things that will help promote a balanced ecosystem.

Site considerations

Your pond's location can affect its ecological balance. A low-lying site, for example, may flood with rainwater or runoff carrying fertilizers, pesticides, or animal waste from your yard or automobile pollutants from your driveway. It might also become a catch basin for blowing leaves. Runoff and fallen leaves both bring unwelcome new elements into the ecosystem and will throw it out of balance. Avoid building your pond at the lowest point in your yard or entirely beneath trees.

Sunlight also affects a pond's ecological balance. The sun promotes growth of aquatic plants and algae and warms the water. Beneficial bacteria are more active when the water temperature is above 50°F. You will sometimes see cloudy "green water" in early spring because the nitrogen cycle is out of balance when the water temperature is cold and the bacteria colonies are not able to keep up with the organic debris and waste. A water garden situated where it receives at least partial sun will be easier to maintain in ecological balance.

Design considerations

Planning ahead can help to create a healthy balance in your water feature. The most successful designs include biological or mechanical filtration, a circulation pump, plants, fish, or some combination of these.

■ **Biological filters** provide surface area where beneficial bacteria can grow. The bacteria

To create a healthy water garden and minimize maintenance, it's helpful to understand the inner workings of a pond ecosystem. An ecosystem is a community of organisms that interact with one another and their environment as a unit. A pond ecosystem includes microorganisms such as algae and bacteria as well as plants and perhaps fish. These work together in the nitrogen cycle, the balance of which determines the health of the water and its inhabitants.

▲ **Fish consume insects and algae but also reduce oxygen and produce waste. Limit their number according to the size of your water garden.**

will form naturally over time, or you can buy some to start a colony more quickly. A pond lined with rock creates the perfect living environment for beneficial bacteria, acting as a giant biological filter. Rock-lined ponds will require periodic power washing to remove built-up algae and bacteria. Although many mechanical filters include biological media where bacteria can grow, they do not provide the volume of a rock lining. Because chlorine kills beneficial bacteria and fish, treat tap water with a chlorine neutralizer before running it through a biological filter.

■ **Mechanical filters** are skimmer boxes that remove large debris and leaves. Locate a skimmer box as far from the waterfall, stream, or other feature as possible. Place it where it can pull water across the pond's surface. Avoid a design that creates a quiet cove of "dead" water because that is often where debris will settle. Ideally, the entire pond will flow toward the skimmer box. Cleaning the mechanical filter is as simple as emptying a catch net once a week. A pond without a mechanical filter must be skimmed with a net each day to remove floating debris before it sinks and clogs the drain or pump. (See pages 46–49 for more information on skimmers and filters.)

■ **Pumps** circulate water through the biological and mechanical filters, which promotes a balanced ecosystem. Splashing water from a falls or fountain adds needed oxygen to the water. For the best balance, a pump must be large enough to circulate the entire volume of water in the pond once every two hours. (See pages 38–42 for more information on pumps.)

◄ **Splashing water adds oxygen to the pond. Circulating water through biological and mechanical filters adds beneficial bacteria and removes harmful debris from your water garden.**

▼ **Plants control algae by shading the water and taking up nitrates for growth. They also add oxygen to the water. If some plants become invasive, reduce their quantity to maintain clear water and keep the fish healthy.**

■ **Fish** are fun to watch and feed, and they also play an important role in the pond's ecosystem. They produce waste and carbon monoxide as well as consume insects, plants, algae, and oxygen. To maintain a healthy balance, avoid overstocking your pond with too many fish. If you stock your pond with no more than 1 inch of goldfish length or ½ inch of koi per 5 gallons of water, you'll leave some room for growth of the fish.

■ **Plants** contribute to a balanced ecosystem in many ways. They provide food for fish, and shade the water surface, which can help control algae. Some species are healthy to the point of being invasive and must be controlled in order to keep water and fish in good condition. Submerged plants, also called oxygenators, remove carbon dioxide and add oxygen to the water during the day, aiding fish and aerobic bacteria. Both plants and algae use nitrates in the water for growth; that competition for nutrients helps control algae.

Keep the potential health of your ecosystem in mind when choosing your site and creating your design, and you'll be rewarded with fewer maintenance tasks and more pond-viewing time.

POND STYLE AND SHAPE

Ponds can take whatever shape your imagination and site allow. There are two basic style categories—formal and informal.

Formal style

Clean, simple, straight lines and symmetrical, mirror-image arrangements characterize formal styles. Formal water gardens have straight edges and geometric shapes. Brickwork makes a functional yet highly decorative border for a formal pond, as do square precast pavers, tile, uniform-size stones, and even sod.

Formal designs work well paired with manicured beds of roses and neat, evenly planted perennial borders accented with clipped boxwood hedges or other small shrubs. If your landscape design is formal and you're considering a reflecting pool—a water feature whose principal function is to reflect trees, sky, or plantings at the edge of the flower border—a square or rectangular shape is just what you're looking for. For lushness, add a large display of water lilies with a towering papyrus.

Informal style

Curving, fluid lines and asymmetrical arrangements define informal design. The American cottage garden or the mixed perennial border dotted here and there with bright colors provides the perfect

▲ **Formal ponds have geometric shapes and straight, simple lines.**

▼ **Informal ponds fit into the curving lines and asymmetrical shapes of nature.**

setting for an informal pond. An informal water garden flows seamlessly, without defined edges, into the surrounding landscape plantings.

In contrast to formal designs where plants are used as ornaments, plants are the heart of the look in informal styles. Foliage of similar texture and form in both the pond and perennial borders casually links the pond with the rest of the landscape. Water garden edging complements—rather than defines—informal style. Large, irregular fieldstone, river rock, or boulders; logs; or pebbles make the pond look as if it has always been part of the landscape.

Pond shapes

Rectangles and squares are typical formal shapes. Because of their straight, simple lines, they work well when you need to define a space, whether the entire garden or part of it.

Oval and circular ponds are difficult to categorize. They may be either formal or informal, depending on their size and edging and the geometry of their plantings. The more a rectangle approaches—but does not become—a circle, the more it will tend to look informal. Soft, planted edges accentuate the effect. A long, narrow, oval pond looks formal because it begins to take on the character of a rectangle as its length becomes more than three times its width. It is best to complement it with the hard, straight edges of cut stone or other formal construction materials.

Free forms, such as crescents or kidney and pie shapes, are informal because of their asymmetrical edges.

◀ Rectangular ponds are easy to line. You will need extra flexible liner to fold and overlap around the curves of a shape with irregular sides.

Circular and oval pond shapes, as well as teardrops and ellipses, are often easier to install when using flexible liner. Because circles and ovals lack corners, the liner is easy to fold.

Free-form designs are the most popular but can also be the most difficult—and the most expensive—to execute because so much liner is taken up in folds and overlaps. These shapes have inner and outer arcs. You'll need to buy enough liner to fit all the outer arcs, which means the inner arcs will have too much liner in them and you'll have to take it up. A crescent-shaped pond can require one-third more liner than a rectangular one of equivalent volume. A pie-shaped pond requires less liner than a crescent of the same size. This extra amount isn't crucial in small ponds, but it can be significant in large ponds.

The final shape of your water feature is determined by the relationship of its size to its edging. Because the proportion of plants and edging predominate in a small feature, these elements influence shape more than the original shape of the hole. You can actually make the right-angled formality of a small rectangular pond disappear by using informal plantings. Larger ponds are harder to blend in. As the size of the excavation increases—to a quarter acre or more, for example—the shape becomes predominant.

Installation considerations

Each pond shape requires different quantities of liner and installation time. The more complicated the shape, the more folds you will need to make in the liner.

Rectangles are one of the easiest styles to install. You have to make only four folds when using flexible liner, so this is the most efficient use of flexible materials.

▲ An informal water garden without defined edges seems to blend seamlessly into the surrounding landscape.

WHICH STYLE IS FOR YOU?

Water features are as individual as the gardeners who create them. Answer the following questions to help you decide which style is best for you.

> Rocks and plants are positioned to make this informal pond appear to have occurred naturally.

What size?

▦ Do you have an hour or two (or more) each week to devote to water gardening?
▦ Is your landscape fairly large?
▦ Have you installed (or helped to install) a water garden before?
▦ Are you experienced with do-it-yourself projects?
▦ Do you have friends or family who can help with installation?
▦ Will your budget allow you spend several hundred dollars or more on a water feature?

If you answered "no" to most of the questions, you should build a small pond.

Formal or informal?

▦ Do you like straight lines and symmetry?
▦ Does your landscape already have a number of formal elements?
▦ Do you thrive on order?
▦ Is your lot a geometric shape?
▦ Do the doors and windows of your house look out on a landscape designed in blocks or grids?
▦ Is your home interior formal?
▦ Do natural gardens seem disorderly or messy to you?

If you answered "yes" to most questions, you may prefer a formal garden pool.

▲ Use drystack masonry in a large, informal setting to create a waterfall that cascades gently into the pond and connects the feature to the surrounding landscape.

▼ An elegant formal style features straight lines and orderly plantings.

To dig, or not to dig?

▦ Will digging the garden be difficult for you?
▦ Would you like the water garden located near a sitting area, and should the water be at eye-level when you're seated?
▦ Is the water table high in your area?
▦ Do you live in an area with a reasonably mild climate?
▦ Is your site in a low spot that might flood if the water feature isn't above ground?

The more "yes" answers, the more an aboveground pool is appropriate for your site; the more "no" answers, the more an in-ground pond is the better choice.

Which features?

▦ Do you want the sound of splashing water?
▦ Will you keep fish in the water garden?
▦ Do you want to see falling water or watch it course through your landscape?
▦ Is your site calm, not buffeted by winds that might disturb a waterfall or other moving water?

If you answered "yes" to most questions, include a fountain, stream, or waterfall in your plans.

Do you want plants?

▦ Will your garden receive four or more hours of sunlight each day?
▦ Are you interested in tending new plants?
▦ Do you want fish?
▦ Are you concerned about keeping the water clear without chemicals?
▦ Are you willing to spend extra time to care for plants?

If you answered "yes" to most questions, add plants to your pond.

Avoid sharp angles and shapes that exhibit the "amoeba syndrome"—lobes extending from the main body of the design. Lobes mean pinches, and pinches mean folds and extra liner. These shapes will be difficult to install and to mow around. Also, the lobes create dead zones in the pond where water can't easily circulate. Pond water settles into these dead areas and reduces oxygen levels, which is harmful to fish and other fauna. Choose simple, straight geometrical shapes for formal gardens. Curving lines, free-form shapes, and asymmetrical plantings look best in informal pond designs.

◀ Combine a simple rock waterfall with a runnel to create a water feature in a formal courtyard. See page 108 for instructions on how to build a runnel.

POND SHAPES

▲ Lobes are hard to install and reduce oxygen.

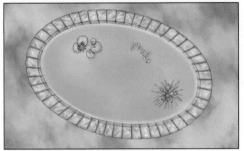

▲ Ovals and circles can be formal or informal, depending on size, edging, and plants.

▲ Use plants of varying size and texture to soften and blend the edges of a symmetrical pond into the surrounding landscape.

Should you have fish in your garden?

▦ Do you live in a mild climate? If not, are you willing to overwinter the fish indoors?
▦ Are you willing to provide the extra weekly care that fish require?
▦ Do you want to minimize mosquitoes?
▦ Is having a complete, self-regulating ecosystem important to you?

If you answered "yes" to most questions, add fish to your pond.

In-ground versus aboveground

In-ground ponds are good projects for beginning water gardeners because their installation generally doesn't require special skills. Aside from digging and hauling soil away, building one is simple—dig it, line it, and fill it. Even when small, an in-ground pond is attractive and fits into both natural and formal landscapes.

Aboveground pools also have advantages but require more installation work. They're excellent for areas where you want the water close to eye level or situated at just the right height for dangling fingers. Aboveground pools are ideal for those difficult-to-dig locations in clay, in compacted soil, or among tree roots. They are suited to mild climates where water doesn't freeze and where footings can be set less thick and deep.

Although some aboveground pools require little digging (others, none at all), most still need sides. Depending on the style you choose, constructing them can take skill. The sides can be built from almost any material: brick, stone, concrete, tile, or wood.

Ponds for fish

Some aboveground pools may be large and deep enough to hold a few koi or goldfish. However, if your water garden is designed with fish as a primary focus, you will need to dig an appropriate-sized in-ground pond.

A fishpond, by definition, is designed to carry a heavier concentration of fish than a smaller water garden. Your site must allow you to dig the pond with a slope toward center drains that remove settling fish

▷ **Build an aboveground pool where you want to bring the water closer to eye level.**

waste or you must install pumps that handle solid waste. It must also be situated so that you have easy access for pump maintenance and removal of floating debris, which are necessary to reduce the chance of fish infection and to increase the quality of the water. A site not too close to permanent utility structures and not under dense foliage can make your efforts easier.

To protect water plants from hungry fish, dig two smaller ponds connected by a stream and isolated from each other by a gate valve or waterfall. Design one pond for aquatic plants and the other as a home for goldfish and koi. The planted pond can function as a miniature wetland, absorbing waste from the fish and cleaning the water. Both ponds will be healthier and easier for you to maintain.

Waterfalls

Waterfalls contribute motion and sound to a landscape. What's more, a waterfall may provide a solution for areas otherwise difficult to landscape, such as steep slopes, rocky terrain, or deep shade. A forceful waterfall helps minimize traffic noise. Whatever water feature you choose, it will set your landscape apart from the ordinary.

Before designing a waterfall, look for inspiration. Take time to observe some of nature's creations. Notice the water basin or area at the top of a falls, how the water spills over and around the rocks, and how far it falls. Visit private or public gardens that have waterfalls, including synthetic ones. Look at photos and artists' renditions of waterfalls. Ask landscape architects or designers to show you installed waterfalls that they created.

▽ **You can keep a few fish in an aboveground pool, but a pond designed for koi does best installed in ground.**

A waterfall looks natural when built on a slope. If your property is level, create changes of level in order to make the water feature appear natural. When you excavate for the feature, save the soil and use it to sculpt low walls, shape the watercourse, or create planting areas around the feature. Be sure to pack and tamp the loose soil around the pond liner and rock work to prevent future settling and damage.

Style and substance

Once you've gathered ideas, incorporate some into your plans and note others to avoid. The style of your waterfall should be obvious now. A formal design might include geometric elements, such as a straight-sided canal, stair-stepped falls, or a wall that water slides over. Popular building materials for formal designs include cut stone, tile, metal, and acrylic. The landscape could include ground covers or tailored trees and shrubs.

An informal or natural waterfall design typically includes a single spillway surrounded by an outcropping of rocks or a rock garden. Or you might opt for a multiple-cataract waterfall, where more than one stream flows over the spillway. The plumbing for this design utilizes a manifold behind the falls that divides the water pipeline from the pump into two or more lines. Each line has its own valve to regulate how much water flows over each part of the waterfall and through the rock face as it discharges water between rocks at the top of the waterfall.

Watercourses consist of a series of basins or small pools linked by cascades or a tiered stream. As water overflows a pool, it either drops directly into a pond or spills onto rocks and into a stream. When two or more pools are connected by a waterfall or stream, design each lower basin of your watercourse larger than the one above it.

As the water recirculates in a watercourse, it is pumped from the lowest pond to fill the uppermost pool to overflowing. The lowest pond should be large enough that when water is pumped out of it to overflow the upper pool, the drop in volume won't be noticeable.

If you design a pond with a waterfall, locate the falls on the far side of the main approach to the pond. Plan on a buffer such as smooth rocks or marginal plants between a turbulent waterfall and the calm waters where water lilies grow.

▲ **Water rushing over a falls and down a steep slope is energizing.**

▼ **Solve the problem of rocky terrain with a falls. It can also mask traffic noise.**

Size matters

A 10×15-foot pool provides enough water to feed a waterfall about 2 feet high. It's possible to plan for five or six falls over several yards. Falls higher than 3 feet should be reserved for large ponds with extremely powerful pumps.

For a small pond, limit your waterfall's height to 1 to 2 feet to keep it natural looking and to limit water loss as it splashes outside of the waterway. Low falls also allow you to use a less-powerful pump to keep the water flowing. This not only saves money when buying a pump but can also result in substantial energy savings as the pump operates.

A low waterfall will still provide the appealing view and soothing sounds of flowing water that attract so many people to water gardening.

▲ **A meandering watercourse with multiple falls at different levels evokes a sense of leisure.**

Streams and bogs

A stream or watercourse typically runs from a waterfall to a pond. However, it can also function completely independently or be teamed up with another element, such as a bog garden. As with a waterfall, design the stream so it looks as though it has occurred naturally. Take as many clues from nature as possible. Check out rocky, gurgling streams in the hills or mountains, and slower, calmer, meandering meadow creeks. Observe how the water flows more quickly where a streambed narrows and slows in wider spots. See how rocks and other obstacles affect current speed and direction. Gather photos of areas that appeal to you. Naturalizing your watercourse with rocks and plants will be essential to making it look as though it is a natural part of your landscape rather than an add-on feature.

Where to begin

If your property has a gentle, natural slope, it should lend itself well to stream construction. Let the stream follow the natural terrain if possible. A streambed approximately level across its width will look natural. If your site provides no natural slope, create one with the soil excavated to make the stream. Compact the soil to prevent settling and structural flaws. Design the stream with an occasional dam so that it holds water when the pump isn't operating. A vertical drop of 1 to 2 inches per 10 feet of length provides adequate flow. If the slope of your proposed stream area drops more steeply, create a series of long pools with vertical drops between them. The higher the vertical drop of water, the larger and deeper the pool under the falls should be to minimize water loss from splashing. In general the pool diameter should be at least twice as wide as the height of the waterfall.

As with any water feature, begin your design with a site plan and sketches depicting the stream's placement and flow direction within your landscape. Keep in mind that a stream is often more interesting if it is not all visible at once. Curves and bends create a natural look—soft, flowing curves rather than quick, sharp turns. Water flows faster on the outside of a curve, and it pushes harder against the outside of the curve than its inside. Avoid long stretches of shallow water because algae will build up if the current is too leisurely. Build the pools at least 12 inches deep if possible.

Placement of natural rock determines the finished appearance of the stream. Plan to acquire a variety of rock sizes and shapes. Use the larger stones to direct and channel water; use smaller pebbles to create a ripple effect as water flows over them. Placing rocks on the outside of the curve creates more turbulence there. Rocks may also be used to decrease the width of the stream, making water flow faster. They also enhance the visual effect, and in some cases add delightful sounds as water rushes by or over them.

Stream layout

Use your site plan or a sketch as a guide to laying out the stream with a hose or rope. Think about where the piping will go. You'll want a straight, direct-as-possible pipeline from the bottom (source) of the

plants that thrive in wet or moist soil.
Known as marginal plants, most grow
best with wet roots, but some adapt to
periodically dry conditions.

plants that thrive in wet or moist soil.
Known as marginal plants, most grow
best with wet roots, but some adapt to
periodically dry conditions.

Bogs can be part of a pond or a separate
aquatic feature. When incorporated into
the edge of a pond with fish, bogs act as
a filter, providing an ideal mechanism for
enhancing the quality of the water. Fish
waste-polluted water recirculating through
the bog carries nutrients to plants and
beneficial bacteria growing there. They
in turn clean the water and enhance the
quality of life in the fishpond.

The beauty of choices

Choosing a water feature is like choosing a
home: the choice has to suit your interests,
who you are, how you spend your time,
and what you expect from your natural
surroundings. A powerful waterfall gives
self-expression and fulfillment to some.
For others, nothing is finer than a gentle
stream flowing to a bog garden and lily
pond. Still others enjoy growing aquatic
plants in a deck or patio water garden.
The beauty is that the choice is yours.

▲ Irises and other
marginal plants
thrive in the boggy
soil at the edge of
the pond.

watercourse to its upper end (head). The
stream's source might be a waterfall, pond,
or plant filter. Or water could appear to
arise out of the ground like a spring flowing
from a bed of rocks; the end of it is usually
a sizeable pond. The water could disappear
into a bed of rocks, disguising the housing
for a pump that returns water to the stream
head. However you design it, the catch
basin should be large enough to hold all
the water when the pump is shut off.

Design one or more places to cross the
stream, depending on length and width.
Options include bridges or stepping-stones.
Consider adding bog gardens filled with
marginal and bog plants adjacent to the
stream. Bog gardens create natural
transitions from the stream to surrounding
dry-garden areas. Bogs look natural when
positioned on the outside edges of bends
in the stream, where they won't interfere
with its flow. The bogs receive water from
the stream to replace whatever is lost
through evaporation.

Bog garden

Constructing a bog garden puts you on
the cutting edge of landscape and garden
designs. Bog gardens not only mimic a
swampy, natural habitat, but they also
present an opportunity to turn a poorly
draining, soggy area into a beautiful garden
teeming with wildlife. For plant lovers, bogs
display a vast array of seldom-seen native

▶ This gentle
stream with a
simple bridge and
bench provides the
perfect spot for
contemplation
and resting.

ATTRACTING WILDLIFE TO THE WATER GARDEN

◄ Songbirds are attracted to the fresh water in a shallow pool. Remember to provide nesting sites and sheltered feeding locations to draw birds to your garden.

Trickling or splashing water in a garden pond is a welcome invitation to birds and butterflies otherwise forced to use roadside puddles. However, many constructed ponds don't adequately meet birds' and butterflies' vital need for water. Often the sides drop away at a sharp angle, making it impossible for small birds to reach the water and presenting too deep a source for butterflies to use. Constructing water features with these creatures in mind will make your pond attractive to and safe for a variety of species.

Design to scale

Add a bathing area to an existing pond by placing a thin flat stone 1 to 3 inches below the water level. Place a scrap of extra pond liner under the stone to prevent damage from sharp edges. Or position a flat-topped rock a bit taller than the water is deep to one edge of a stream. As moving water splashes past, droplets will collect on the rock's surface. Small birds and butterflies will appreciate your effort.

To create a hummingbird-sized water feature, install a small pump and misting hose where it will spray across an exposed flat rock. Hummers will delight in flying through the spray and sipping from the small indentations on the rock.

Butterflies drink from only the shallowest of puddles, hoping to keep their wings dry. Create a butterfly drinking station by filling a shallow flowerpot saucer with smooth river rocks. Place it at or slightly above ground level among some blooming plants. Fill it with fresh, cool water just to the point where water is visible between the rocks but does not cover them all. This leaves dry places on the rocks for sure footing while the butterflies sip.

Add a beach

Add a pebble beach to create a natural-looking, safe spot for birds to walk on. A gentle slope into the water provides a variety of water depths for different-sized birds. Dig the pond with this in mind and purchase enough liner to cover the extended area. (If your pond is already in place, you can use liner tape to seam an extra piece onto the existing edge.)

A POOL TO ATTRACT WILDLIFE

A pebble beach's gentle slope lets animals approach water gradually

Floating plants shade water and provide landing pads for insects

Rock basking places attract butterflies to warm themselves

Trees and shrubs attract beneficial insects, and provide wildlife food and cover

Food for water fowl includes duckweed and duck potato

Grasses provide cover near water year-round

Rock nooks and crannies give amphibians cool spots in summer and hibernation spots in winter

Wildlife-attracting marginal and bog plants provide food and nectar for a wide variety of animals

Provide foliage and flowers

Vary the heights and textures of plants in your garden to attract the widest variety of birds. Tree branches above the pond allow birds to pause and check for predators before flying down for a drink. Leafy canopies and brushy shrubs provide safe places to retreat and preen. Tall grasses and other marginal plants offer insect-eating birds a place to forage. Plants with berries and prominent seed heads will guarantee visits from songbirds.

Hummingbirds are particularly drawn to trumpet-shaped blooms. Among their favorites are honeysuckle, trumpet vine, cardinal flower, lantana, columbine, fuchsia, and impatiens. Flowering shrubs, such as azaleas, weigela, and quince, and flowering trees, such as crab apple and tulip poplar, will entice them too. The blossoms provide nectar and also attract insects that make up the balance of a hummingbird's diet.

Butterflies also collect nectar from a variety of flowering plants, but some species prefer or require a specific type. Likewise, most butterfly caterpillars need a specific kind of host plant. For a garden that butterflies will find most appealing, use both host plants and nectar plants. Check on the Internet or at the library for a list of plants best suited to butterflies in your area.

Avoid using pesticides in a water garden designed to attract wildlife. Such products are not specific about which bugs they kill, and will eliminate desirable insects such as butterflies too. Also, pesticide runoff into the pond can kill fish. Let the birds eat any insect pests, and the fish can take care of the mosquitoes.

Dig out an area at the side of your pond at least 2 feet square. Leave the outer edge at the same height as the ground and make a gradual slope toward the pond that increases in depth no more than 1 inch for every 8 inches of distance. Dig the inner edge of the beach approximately 5 to 8 inches below the pond's water level.

Cover the excavated area with the flexible liner. Along the deep edge, place a row of stones large enough to keep pebbles from rolling into the water. Fill in the beach area with enough pebbles or sand to create a maximum water depth of 3 inches. Add flat edging stones at the perimeter to provide a landing and preening area.

At the shallowest side of the beach, create a pint-sized puddle in a shallow indentation safely away from gushing or rapidly moving water. Add just enough water to keep the sand or pebbles wet. If possible, position this miniature water feature so that it collects water droplets from your pond's waterfall or fountain spray. Puddle visitors may include swallowtails, whites, sulphurs, blues, brushfoots, admirals, and skippers.

Some male butterflies need to drink from mud puddles in order to replenish the salts their bodies need for reproduction. Create a butterfly puddle using mud instead of sand or pebbles in order to help them perform this essential function. Expect to be rewarded with visits from such mud-puddling butterflies as whites, sulphurs, and swallowtails.

▲ **Butterflies will drink from small, shallow puddles or even from droplets on rocks positioned away from rapidly moving water. Place a few rocks in but not covered by the water to provide sure footing.**

▶ **Swallowtail butterflies find the nectar irresistible in the late-summer blooms of Joe-Pye weed.**

FINISHING TOUCHES

Just as with a new home, when construction on your water feature is complete, it will be time to move your furnishings in and decorate. Your pond or stream may look raw and out of place in the landscape at first but will quickly become natural as you add plants and a few personal touches.

Plants

Choose aquatic and water-loving marginal plants based on the site and scale of your water garden and your geographical area. If your water garden will be in a new landscape, add a variety of shrubs and perennials grouped in drifts along paths around the pond's perimeter. If you are building your water feature into an existing garden, plan to link the landscape elements together with plants that provide a transition from water to dry land. Leave a few open areas for viewing along the water's edge, but don't be afraid to obscure parts of the pond—especially any mechanical or construction areas you want to hide—behind large plants.

Ornaments

Decorate the garden with accents that reflect your personal style and the type of water feature you have built. Often, a single ornamental element tucked into lush plantings at the water's edge can catch the eye and add character, charm, or even whimsy. For example, position a lighthearted garden gnome or concrete frog under a knee-high plant canopy. Visitors who come upon it peeking up from the plants will take delight in the discovery.

Or consider a colorful container or birdbath. Shop tag sales or architectural

▲ Tuck a favorite piece of sculpture at the edge of a bog to surprise visitors and add a touch of whimsy.

▼ As summer fades into autumn, marginal plants and deciduous trees that change color as they mature add visual interest to the garden. Some aquatic plants are at their most attractive even after the first frost.

salvage stores for old pots and basins that can be put to new use. Or find contemporary sculptures and birdbaths in a variety of styles at home improvement stores and garden centers. New concrete items can be quickly aged with stain products if desired. With a little attention to scale, almost any artifact can be incorporated on the banks of your pond. Ornaments from the size of a baseball to ones even 3 or 4 feet tall will blend agreeably in the design of an average-sized home pond. Unless your water garden is quite large, avoid life-size statues that might detract from the real focal point of the water feature.

Stepping-stones and lights

Some design elements, such as stepping-stones, lights, benches, or a bridge, add both form and function to your water garden. A stepping-stone path across a bubbling stream is an inviting and useful accent. Soft landscape lighting can help you safely find your way to sit on a bench at the pond's edge after dark. Aim a miniature spotlight at the waterfall for sparkle at night.

Remember that once your pond is built, the bulk of the work will be done. You can easily add and remove plants as the garden matures, and you can always move or replace ornaments and lights to create the style you want.

A DESIGN CHECKLIST

Size things up

Before you dig, measure carefully to be sure you'll end up with the correct size and depth. A pond that is too small or too shallow or too deep will make it hard to care for aquatic life. Ask other pondkeepers what depth works best for water gardening in your climate.

Make your pond as large as you can for the space you have available. If you must start out small with an in-ground pond, use a flexible liner so that you can add on later. Double-check your measurements to be sure you have at least 2 feet of overlap along the edge of the pond. Stones, plants, or other edging will hide the excess, while splashing water is kept where it belongs.

Multiply the total volume of your pond (surface length × surface width × depth) by 7.5 to determine the approximate number of gallons of water it will hold. It's surprising how many gallons it takes to fill a square foot of space. A half whiskey barrel, for example, holds about 25 gallons of water. A typical backyard pond may hold 250 to 1,000 gallons or more.

Check your math

Make sure your stream or waterfall is in proportion to the main pond. The calculations take some thought, but are crucial to making good equipment choices. The amount of water used by a feature will drain down the pond by the same amount when the feature is running, and fill it up when the feature is turned off.

◀ **Design a pool or pond in scale with its surroundings. Measure carefully so that you dig the correct shape to the right depth.**

◀ **Double-check your calculations to be certain you choose the right-sized pump to power your recirculating water feature, such as this double waterfall.**

Use your calculations to choose the right pump for the features you want to power. Pick one no smaller in size than one-third the total gallons of water in the pond. There are many inexpensive pumps available, but they may have hidden costs, depending on your design. A low-capacity pump may not be powerful enough to run a waterfall, or may be expensive to use because it isn't energy-efficient. An efficient pump that costs a bit more but comes with a good warranty is a better investment.

Keep elements in balance

Choose materials and plants that blend well with existing elements on your site. A water garden should fit in with the rest of your landscape. An isolated pond ringed with nearly identical large stones can look harsh or out of place in an otherwise natural setting. Choose edging materials that coordinate with those of your patio or deck. Soften the perimeter with marginal plants that help to tie the water garden to terrestrial areas of your yard. Be sure to include enough aquatic plants to help balance the pond's ecosystem. Submerged plants will help to control algae growth by adding oxygen to the water, while marginal plants can help by keeping some surface areas shaded and cooler.

A certain amount of algae is unavoidable. When living things are present, the water will become cloudy, and clarity will change with the season. Algae and cloudiness are normal, healthy signs of a thriving water garden. Monitor water quality and algae growth to keep them in balance. Because you have designed your pond for easy maintenance, these tasks should be simple.

MATERIALS & EQUIPMENT

Water gardening has been revolutionized by new materials that make it easier than ever to create a feature that's perfect for your landscape. Not so long ago, creating any kind of water feature meant you had to hire professionals to form and reinforce a concrete watercourse and install complex plumbing and electrical systems. Today, there's an entirely new way to create water gardens.

Flexible and preformed liners have replaced the concrete. Now you can install most water features yourself—without professional help—in an unending variety of shapes, sizes, and styles.

Pumps install with little effort, use regular household current, and recirculate the water (there's no more need for special plumbing). Fountains attach easily to their supporting structures. Filters (which once had to be installed out of the water) are now often attached to the pumps. With simplified techniques and equipment, it's possible to install a small water feature in just a weekend.

Although the materials have been revolutionized, the essential equipment remains the same. A spade, wheelbarrow, carpenter's level, measuring tape, and heavy leather gloves are the basic tools you'll need to complete your garden pond project.

Make sure all tools are clean, repaired, and in excellent condition before you begin. Sharpen your spade, tighten the wheelbarrow bolts, and inflate its tire.

The proper materials and supplies, after all, will help you avoid problems as you easily execute your project to produce professional-looking results.

▼ **Just a few basic tools and some water garden items are all you need to get started.**

LINERS

One of the most important innovations in garden pond technology is flexible liner. Developed in the 1960s to replace poured concrete and other building materials, it allows you to create pools, streams, and waterfalls in almost any shape, length, and style you can imagine.

Flexible liner will help you build water gardens in places not possible before. Line an aboveground brick garden pool, for example, or waterproof a whiskey barrel half. Make an artificial stream with sand, gravel, and stones arranged on the liner. Restore a leaky concrete pond by draining it and laying liner over the damaged concrete.

Flexible liners are made from polyvinyl chloride (PVC), polyethylene, and ethylene propylene diene monomer (EPDM). Though the majority sold today are 45-mil EPDM, they vary in thickness, cost, and quality. Heavier liners will generally be more expensive, more durable, and more puncture- and tear-resistant than lighter weight liners. However, new liner developments combine durability with lighter weight. As a rule, the more you spend, the more the liner will resist the sun's ultraviolet rays.

UV light is the constant enemy of liner material (especially polyethylene). It breaks down the chemical bonds in the liner, making it brittle and prone to ripping and splitting. If you plan to build your garden pond with polyethylene flexible liner, remember to keep the pond filled with water and the liner completely covered so none of it is exposed.

Most liner comes in black, a color well-suited to garden pools. Black looks natural and blends with the algae that tend to cover it after a few months.

▲ Flexible liner is so easy to use that one person can install a small water garden with little effort. The time-consuming task is folding and tucking the excess liner.

Black also helps the liner resist UV damage and gives a pool or pond the illusion of greater depth.

Stock sizes for liners start with 5-foot squares and range up to sections 50×100 feet or more. You can join pieces with liner tape or seam sealer made specifically for this purpose to create streams and other large features.

When buying a liner, make sure it is made for use with plants and fish. Liners for other uses (swimming pools or roofs, for example) will be toxic to living things.

Underlayment

All liners require the installation of an underlayment, a cushion layer of material between the liner and the soil that prevents punctures and tears. Sand is a good choice for the pool bottom and other horizontal surfaces but can't be laid vertically. Newspaper is acceptable but deteriorates over time. Old carpet and specially made pond underlayment (which resembles sheets of fiberglass insulation) are ideal.

HOW TO DETERMINE THE LINER SIZE

Purchase a flexible liner by the square foot. Determine the size of your water feature before you purchase a liner for it.

HERE'S HOW:
Imagine your pond as a rectangle, even though it may be round or irregular. Make sure the rectangle includes the farthest points of the pond. Then consider how deep the pond will be. The liner size equals the length (l) plus two times the depth (d), plus 2 feet, multiplied by the width (w) plus two times the depth (d), plus 2 feet. This allows a 1-foot margin all the way around the perimeter. Professionals often add only 6 inches around the perimeter, leaving little margin for error. Avoid the risk of having to patch on extra later by leaving a 1-foot margin now.

A pond whose imaginary rectangle measures 15 feet by 10 feet and is 1½ feet deep needs a liner 20 feet (15 + 1½ + 1½ + 2 = 20) by 15 feet (10 + 1½ + 1½ + 2 = 15); 20×15 = a 300-square-foot liner.

Make any number of depth and surface configurations, including shelves, with a given-size liner; the same formula applies.

At this point, don't worry about figuring the volume (number of gallons) your water feature will hold. Some suppliers give the maximum gallons possible using their liner (or other product) and assuming a given depth. You will need the volume in order to determine the fish-carrying capacity and to figure the appropriate size of optional features such as a waterfall, pump, mechanical filter, UV clarifier, and water treatments.

Figure the volume of a pond or other feature by multiplying its cubic feet (length × width × depth), then multiplying the number of cubic feet by 7.5 (because each cubic foot contains 7.5 gallons of water).

To size a liner for a finished excavation, measure the length and width of the excavation, using a flexible tape. Add 2 feet to each measurement. Unpack a liner only when you're certain it's the right size.

◀ **Flexible liner conforms to your one-of-a-kind creation. Piece it together as you go. Here, overlapped sections create a streamed flowing into a pond.**

HINT

To make sure there are no sharp rocks that might puncture the liner, walk barefoot or in socks (carefully) over the bottom of the excavated area.

A few new liners are manufactured with an underlayment already attached. They are extremely puncture-resistant and should be used over coarse gravel or sharp rock, for example, or in locations where punctures from tree roots are likely.

Liner tears or punctures are no cause for alarm. You can repair them with a patch and solvent cement or special liner adhesive. However, you'll have to drain the pond first, clean the area, and let it dry so the patch will stick to the liner.

▲ **Once the flexible liner is in place and the pond partially filled, work the liner into the crevices around the sides.**

COMPARING FLEXIBLE LINER MATERIALS

Liner Material	Cost	Advantages	Disadvantages	Comments
Polyethylene	35 cents per square foot and more.	Inexpensive. Most hardware and home supply outlets carry it.	Low-density polyethylene is acceptably durable, but avoid high-density polyethylene. Either can be stiff in cold weather. Polyethylene is difficult to repair.	Purchase black, not transparent. Lasts only about two years in a pond. Will last indefinitely, however, when used in a bog garden where it's not exposed to sun.
PVC (polyvinyl chloride)	50 cents per square foot and more.	Moderately durable; sometimes carries a 10-year warranty. Widely available.	PVC for swimming pools and roofs can be toxic to fish and plants.	20- to 32-mil thicknesses.
EPDM (ethylene propylene diene monomer)	60 cents per square foot and more.	Very durable; usually carries a 20-year warranty. Stays flexible even in cold weather. Very resistant to UV light damage.	More expensive.	Look for EPDM-SF, which is not toxic to fish and plants and is available in 45-mil thickness.
Butyl rubber (synthetic rubber)	80 cents per square foot and more.	Very durable, sometimes lasting up to 50 years. Usually carries a 20-year warranty. Is more elastic than PVC and polyethylene. Stays flexible even in cold weather.	Most expensive. Can be difficult to find.	Generally sold in 30- or 60-mil thicknesses.

▲ This pond and waterfall kit contains the basic supplies you'll need to build your own water garden—underlayment, a flexible liner, filters, a submersible pump, flexible tubing, sealants, and chloramine remover. You supply the decorative rocks, plants, and fish to complete the picture.

Flexible liners

Flexible liner is relatively easy to install. A water gardener can work alone lining a small pond. You may require help from several people to spread liner out evenly in a larger project.

You'll find that flexible liner comes with one drawback that preformed liners don't have: You won't be able to avoid folds and creases. As you fill the pond, you'll have to neatly tuck the liner—especially if it's made of less elastic polyethylene or PVC—into uneven places so the weight of the water won't stress it unevenly and weaken or tear it. This can be difficult to do but will be easier if you let the liner warm in the sun an hour or two before you start work.

FOUNDATION UNDER A BOULDER

Large boulders at the edge of a pond (or in the midst of it) require a concrete support with extra layers of flexible liner and underlayment to prevent leaks.

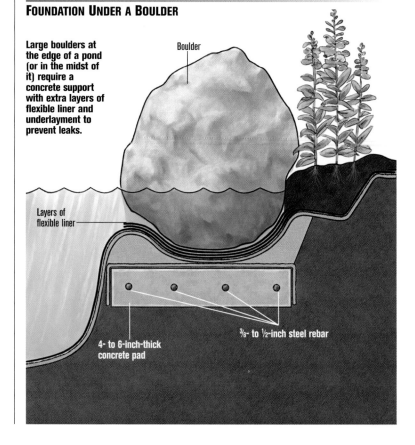

Boulder

Layers of flexible liner

4- to 6-inch-thick concrete pad

⅜- to ½-inch steel rebar

▷ Preformed liners come in various shapes and sizes that allow you to design an aquascape to suit most garden styles. You can create a substantial water garden by combining several small liners in multiple layers with cascades or falls in between.

Preformed liners

Easy to install and well-suited to small garden ponds, preformed liners (also called rigid liners) are available in many ready-made sizes and styles.

Most preformed liners are constructed of fiberglass or rigid plastic. Fiberglass is more expensive but lasts longer than rigid plastic. The price of a 6×3-foot fiberglass liner starts at around $300 (compared with $100 for a rigid-plastic liner); large fiberglass liners can cost $900 or more. Properly installed, a fiberglass liner can last as long as 50 years.

Whether fiberglass or plastic, preformed liners are much more durable than flexible liner and are easier to repair if damaged.

Rigid units have another distinct advantage over flexible liners—they make aboveground water gardens easier to install. They are ideal in areas where stony soil or tree roots prevent or hinder excavation. You can place them either entirely above ground or install them at any depth. But don't expect them to support themselves unless they are high-quality fiberglass. Aboveground ponds will need a structure built around them.

In-ground preformed liners are especially practical for paved areas where the edges can be supported. Rigid liners are available in many shapes, both formal and informal.

HINT

A minimum of 2 inches of soil mixed with sand backfilled under and around a preformed pond will help prevent winter cracking and splitting.

And if the available ready-made shapes don't suit you, shop around for a manufacturer to custom make one for you.

Standard preformed liners also come in various depths. Some include shallow ledges for marginal plants and deep zones for fish to overwinter. For large water gardens—those more than 12 feet long—you can purchase preformed liners in sections that you bolt together and seal with marine silicone. Such sectional liners can be hard to find, however, and require considerably more work. It's better to shop around until you find an existing shape that's right for your landscape.

Although you can buy preformed units in different colors, black is usually best for the same reasons as it is for flexible liners: It's neutral and creates the illusion that the pond is deeper than it actually is.

Make sure the preformed liner is absolutely level and that you backfill nooks and crevices so the plastic doesn't collapse under the weight of the water. Also, you have to be careful about using heavy edging, such as stone. Because some preformed liner edges are convex, the weight of stone will crush them. Other edges are designed to bear weight (check with the supplier) but must be fully supported with backfill.

CONCRETE

I f properly constructed, concrete pools last for decades. However, concrete construction is more difficult and costly than the alternatives. Building a concrete pond may require hiring professionals who have the necessary expertise and tools. Ideally, concrete should be embedded with heavy-duty steel wire mesh or reinforcing rods (rebar) for stability and durability. Gunite, concrete sprayed on steel reinforcing rods, efficiently forms a naturalistic pond. Concrete blocks, concrete and stone, bricks, or decorative tiles offer additional building options, particularly for aboveground water features.

Mortar, a form of concrete, is used for building with blocks or bricks and making seals between them as well as for embedding stone, brick, or comparable edging materials. Mortar tends to separate after repeated freezing and thawing. Alternatively, you may use black urethane foam. It forms a lasting seal that helps prevent leaking because it expands when applied and won't deteriorate over time.

Compacted clay-bottom ponds hold water naturally. They are constructed on

▲ **Concrete ponds lend an old-fashioned feel to a water garden. They are costlier and require more effort to install but will last for many years if properly constructed.**

land with clay-based soil or built with clay that's brought to the site. Their water-holding capacity is sometimes enhanced by adding bentonite, a powdered clay made from volcanic ash.

The digging will be easier in sandy soil, but extra effort is required to be sure the walls are adequately supported. Using both liner and concrete reinforced with wire mesh makes the strongest base. Rebar along the sides anchors the liner and mesh on the wall forms. Be sure to keep some of the excavated soil for backfilling later.

HOW MUCH CONCRETE?

If you want to order enough concrete ready-mix (delivered by a contractor) to make 6-inch-thick walls that withstand a cold climate, use this formula. First, measure the outside dimensions (width × height) of each wall and the pond's bottom; then add the five numbers to determine the total area in square feet. Multiply the total by the thickness of the concrete (6 inches = 0.5 feet) to determine the number of cubic feet. Divide this number by 27 to conclude how many cubic yards of concrete to order. Estimate for a curved or irregular-shape pond by using an imaginary rectangle to figure the area and adding a 10 percent margin of error.

IN COLD CLIMATES

To ensure its success, build a poured-concrete pond as you would a swimming pool. The walls and base must be at least 6 inches thick. Pour or spray concrete all at once (with no seams) over steel reinforcement until you achieve the required thickness.

Concrete ponds

Most ponds were made of concrete until the 1960s, when flexible liners presented a less costly, easier-to-install option. Poured concrete and concrete block are classic-looking building materials that can last decades. Conversely, concrete's high cost and challenging construction make it daunting for an inexperienced builder. If improperly installed, a concrete pool will crack, leak, and cause endless frustration. Avoid using concrete to line a stream. It's expensive and doesn't look natural.

If you prefer, combine the beauty and durability of concrete with a flexible or preformed liner. The liner eliminates the need to neutralize the concrete before adding plants or fish. If the concrete cracks, it won't leak. Also consider finishing a concrete-lined pond with a handsome exterior framework of brick, treated wood, or tile. Capping concrete walls with brick, stone, or pavers gives a pond a stylish look as well.

REINFORCED CONCRETE PERIMETER COLLAR

A concrete collar supports the rock edging around a pond and reinforces the edge's stability.

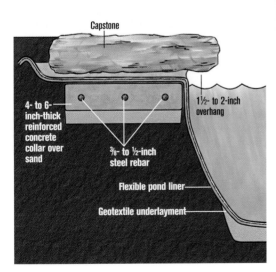

Capstone

4- to 6-inch-thick reinforced concrete collar over sand

1½- to 2-inch overhang

⅜- to ½-inch steel rebar

Flexible pond liner

Geotextile underlayment

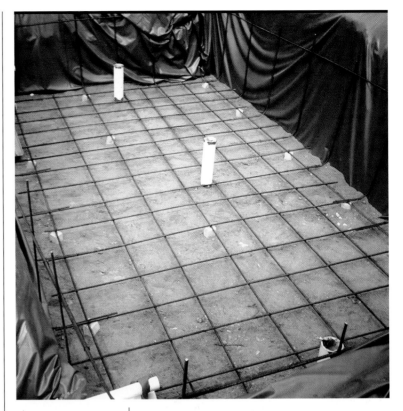

▲ Digging a pond in sandy soil is easier than in heavy clay, but you'll need to use both flexible liner and wire-reinforced concrete to support the base. Anchor the walls with rebar.

Poured concrete or blocks

A poured-concrete structure requires preparing an excavation site and wood forms to shape the walls and hold the concrete while it sets. The base and sides of the excavation should be firmly tamped. Cover the level base with a 4- to 6-inch layer of gravel to help prevent cracking. Sandwich wire mesh or steel rods in between two layers of poured concrete to provide reinforcement and strength. Alternatively, have a professional spray the wire-reinforced form with layers of gunite or shotcrete. You can paint the inside of a concrete pool with a waterproof sealant labeled for water gardens.

Concrete blocks offer a simpler way to construct a pond. Stacked hollow blocks, reinforced with metal rods and filled with concrete, make a formidable structure. Build shelves for plants by shaping the excavation to support them or stacking additional blocks along the pond wall. Line the pond with a flexible or preformed liner. Top the edges with mortared block, brick, or stone.

In regions with cold winters and freeze-thaw cycles, the sides of a concrete pool should slope outward by about 20 degrees overall to allow water in the pool to freeze and expand without cracking the concrete.

PUMPS

HINT

Here's an easy way to calculate the volume of your pond after you've dug and lined it. Jot down the reading on your water meter. Then fill the garden pond and note the new reading. Most meters measure the amount of water used in cubic feet. Convert it to gallons by multiplying by 7.5.

▲ Plastic housing protects an external pump from the elements. Use marginal plants at the pond's edge to camouflage the pump from view.

ANATOMY OF A PUMP

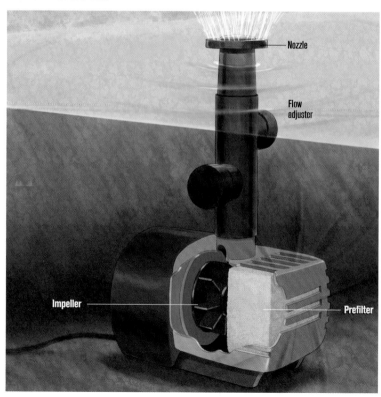

Nozzle

Flow adjuster

Impeller

Prefilter

Still water in a garden pool is beautiful in its own right. But moving water is what adds that splash and sparkle to your water garden. For that, you'll need a pump.

Pumps make streams run, fountains spray, ponds drain, and water recirculate so that waterfalls keep falling. Moving water through a water feature once required complicated plumbing. Today, all you need is a pump. Installation isn't complicated, taking just minutes to assemble and set in your pond.

Submersible or external?

Pumps are available in submersible and external models. In both the mechanism is simply a set of whirling blades that pressurize the water and force it into motion. Submersible pumps are easier to use than external pumps. They sit directly in the water and are inexpensive, unlike external pumps that you must place outside the pond. Submersible pumps are easy to install, start without priming, and run quietly. They can be used to power all but the largest water features.

Before buying a pump for your garden pool or waterfall, check its energy-efficiency rating. Large water features require more pump capacity and thus consume more electric energy.

Look for magnetic-driven pumps, which use less energy than direct-driven pumps. Generally the most efficient pumps are also the most expensive but can pay for themselves in energy efficiency.

Pump size

The most important consideration when choosing which pump to buy is its size. Equipment manufacturers rate electrical power in amps or watts. However, the critical measure of pump power is the number of gallons of water it will pump per hour to a specific height, called the head.

To determine the size pump you'll need, first calculate the volume of water in the pond (see the box at right). As a rule, choose a pump that can move half the total volume in an hour. For example, if your pond holds 500 gallons of water, buy a pump that delivers at least 250 gallons per hour (gph).

If your water garden will include a waterfall or stream, it will need a more powerful pump. Pumps have to work harder to move water up a slope or to the head of the stream. (If you're installing a filter as well, you may need to install a separate pump for it.) Figuring how much more power you'll need is somewhat more complicated. In general, the pump should be able to turn over the total volume of water in an hour. To learn more about measuring gph, see page 41.

When in doubt, buy a more powerful pump. You can restrict flow with a valve (either self-contained or one installed expressly for this purpose). When shopping for a pump for a stream or waterfall, make sure its head capacity, or lift, is well above the height you've planned for your falls.

Other considerations

Pumps have varying lengths of cord; check to make sure the cord is long enough to go through the pond and plug in well away from the water. The longer the better, especially since some codes specify that the electrical outlet for a water feature has to be

see page 41.

FIGURING THE VOLUME OF FIVE DIFFERENT POOL SHAPES

For all shapes, the dimensions should be in feet. After calculating the area of the pond, multiply the result by the average depth of the pool. Then multiply that result by 7.5 to get volume in gallons.

RECTANGLE OR SQUARE:
■ Multiply the length by the width to find area.

OVAL:
■ Measure from center to most distant edge, then from center to nearest edge. Multiply the first figure by the second and the result by 3.14 to find area.

CIRCLE:
■ Measure the radius (the length in feet from center to the edge).
■ Multiply the radius by itself and then by 3.14 to get area.

ABSTRACT, IRREGULAR, AND OBLONG:
■ Break abstract and irregular shapes into simpler units (here, two circles and a rectangle), then calculate the area of each. If that doesn't work, multiply the maximum length by the maximum width to find the pool's area.
■ For an oblong, figure the area by breaking it into a square and two half circles. Calculate the area of the square. Then consider the two half circles as one and calculate its area.

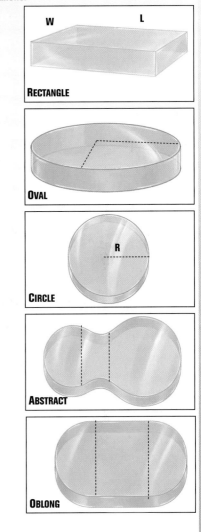

---

at least 6 feet away from water. Avoid extension cords if possible. If you have to use one, make sure it's made for outdoor use and is plugged into a ground fault circuit interrupter (GFCI), a device that shuts off an outlet immediately if there is an overload.

Some pumps come equipped with prefilters. If you need a filter, you can determine what type to get by reading pages 48–51.

Be sure to buy a pump that is designed for use in a water garden. Unlike other types of pumps, those for water gardens are made to sustain round-the-clock use.

▲ **When deciding which pump to purchase, match the volume and lift of your water garden with the capacity of the pump.**

Making the right choice

The splashing music of water as it moves and recirculates adds to the appeal of a water feature. It takes the right size pump to move water from a pool through tubing or pipes and other equipment to a waterfall, fountain, or stream. You need to know how you plan to use a pump in order to choose the right type and size for the job as well as how water will flow and how much resistance it will meet along the way.

■ **Ease the selection by answering these questions:**

■ What kind of water feature do you envision? How will you use the pump? How many gallons per hour (gph) will it require?

■ What size is the water feature? How much water will flow through the pump? How many gph are needed to operate the feature?

■ What else will the pump do? Will it recirculate water through a filter, through a fountain, over a waterfall, or in a stream?

■ For features where water returns downhill to the pond, how high above the water surface is the point where water discharges in a waterfall? What is the width of water flowing over the spillway? How thick a sheet of water do you want going over the spillway?

■ What are the requirements of the filtering system? How many gph does it take to properly operate the filter?

■ Will your feature include fish? If so, how many and what size? A big fish population indicates the need for a biological filter. After deciding on a filter, ask how many gph are needed to operate the biofilter.

HOW TO INTERPRET PUMP CHARACTERISTICS

Model number: Identify a pump by the manufacturer's model number. It remains the same from dealer to dealer and helps you with comparison shopping.

GPH: Calculate how many gallons per hour you need, given the horizontal plus the vertical distance that the recirculating water will flow between the pump and the point where water exits its pipeline. Purchase a pump with a capacity (gph) that's greater than required.

Head (lift): Head is the vertical distance that the pump forces water in the line. Horizontal distance is converted to equivalent head at the rate of 10 feet of horizontal distance to 1 foot of vertical lift.

Maximum head: At the pump's specified maximum head, it no longer recirculates water. Buy a pump with a head height above the total height of the waterfall.

Pump outlet: Water exits the pump, and the water line is attached to the pump at the pump outlet. Its diameter determines the diameter of the line that carries water from the pump to its discharge point. When the horizontal distance of the line exceeds 15 feet, use a fitting to increase the discharge connection to the next larger pipe size.

Amps and watts: Calculate the amount of electricity needed and the approximate cost of running a specific pump based on your local utility rates. Generally, higher numbers translate to higher electrical usage and higher operating expense. Here's a formula: watts × 24 hours (in a day) × 30 days (in a month) ÷ 1,000 = number of kilowatts per month × cost per kilowatt hour = total monthly cost of operating a pump.

■ If your design includes a fountain, how many gph are required to operate the type and height of fountain you chose?

When shopping for a pump consider the following characteristics:

■ How many gph does it recirculate at the height and horizontal distance required?

■ How much electricity does it use?

■ How long is it guaranteed to last?

■ How much does it cost?

The power consumption of pumps varies so much that an energy-efficient model can save enough electricity to pay for itself in one or two seasons of operation. Compare the amperage (amps) and wattage (watts) of competing pumps to determine relative efficiency of energy consumption. The lower the amps and watts, the less electricity a pump consumes.

Measuring gallons per hour

As a pump pushes water higher in a vertical pipe, gravity creates increased resistance. Therefore the gph of a pump decreases as the discharge height (known as head or lift) increases. The resistance created by forcing water to flow horizontally 10 feet is roughly equivalent to the effect of lifting the water 1 foot vertically. If your pump forces water 20 feet horizontally, for example, that translates to 2 feet vertically. Knowing this gph at a designated point tells you whether the pump can deliver the quantity of water needed to properly operate a waterfall with the planned spillway's width, depth, and height as well as its distance from the pump.

Manufacturers list how many gph a pump recirculates at 1 foot of lift and at other heights. If the height you need is between two listed heights, estimate what you could reasonably expect. For example, if you need 300 gph released 3 feet above the water's surface, look for a pump rated at least 300 gph at 3 feet of head. That same pump might recirculate only 200 gph at 6 feet of lift. It would not be powerful enough to recirculate 300 gph for a 6-foot-high waterfall.

To build in a margin of error, measure the water distance vertically from the pump, not from the water's surface. One way or another, avoid skimping on gph. When determining the proper flow rate for a waterfall or stream, figure 150 gph for each inch of spillway width. This rate provides a ½-inch-thick sheet of water over the falls. You'll also need to know how far the water must travel horizontally in the

HOW TO ESTIMATE WATERFALL FLOW

Use a ¾-inch diameter garden hose to test what your new waterfall will look like before investing in a pump for it. This test assumes water pressure at the tap measures 40 to 60 pounds per square inch (normally found in municipal water systems). The hose produces a flow rate of 800 to 900 gph, assuming no nozzle or other restriction. Let the hose discharge at its maximum rate where you plan to have the water line from the pump discharge water. After observing the effect of this rate on your newly constructed waterfall, decide if you want to keep the flow rate at 800 to 900 gph or adjust it higher or lower.

pipeline. Remember that each 10 feet of horizontal distance creates about as much resistance against the pump as 1 foot of head. Consider a pump that must force water 10 feet in a pipe across the pond bottom and then 5 feet up the pipe to the release point in the waterfall. This is equivalent to a 6-foot head.

Although some variation exists from rated gph capacity, pumps do not operate at more than their rated gph capacity for each rated height. To be safe, purchase a pump with greater capacity than estimated need. While a pump's gph cannot be increased, it is easily reduced using a valve on the pipeline or a restrictor clamp on the flexible tubing that limits the flow of water from the pump to the discharge point. Some pumps come with a built-in valve on the discharge. Any restriction you add should be placed on the water line only after the water exits the pump—never before entering the pump. Pumps easily withstand this restriction. It has the same effect as making the pump push the water higher in the line.

▲ A submersible pump is designed to handle the requirements of a system with a biological filter and a waterfall.

The best pump for your water feature

Unless you plan to have an extremely large waterfall or stream, use a submersible pump. Residential water features usually employ submersible pumps of less than 4,000 gph. They provide noiseless operation and ease of setup, giving them a distinct advantage over nonsubmersible (external) pumps. Submersible pumps usually feature a screen intake that protects them from clogging. Some models include a built-in filter and work well for most small fountains, waterfalls, and streams.

Buy the highest-quality pump that you can afford. Bronze, brass, and stainless steel models are reliable and will withstand heavy use over the years. Cast iron and aluminum pumps offer moderate prices and quality compared to the least-expensive plastic models. Select a pump with a cord that's long enough to reach the nearest GFCI electrical outlet. If the outlet lacks GFCI protection, use an outdoor extension cord that has a built-in GFCI.

Unless the submersible pump is designed to handle solids, place it on a platform of bricks or flat rocks a few inches above the pond bottom. This keeps the pump above sediment that accumulates on the pond floor and makes it easier to clean the pump.

Choose from oil-filled or magnetically driven submersible pumps. The latter have a longer life than oil-filled pumps and consume substantially less energy than other pumps. Oil-filled pumps are normally required for high head requirements. Beware of the potential of contaminating leaks from oil-filled pumps. Avoid low-priced residential sump pumps, even though they have an attractive gph rating. They typically burn out from continuous operation within a few months.

Nonsubmersible pumps

Use nonsubmersible pumps for large water features using more than 12,000 gph or in high-output situations, such as waterfalls, requiring a high lift. External models make more noise and are more expensive to operate than submersible pumps. However, they are easier to access for maintenance and cost less initially. A complex plumbing installation may require a professional's assistance. These units must be kept dry and well-ventilated within a protective housing. Be sure to screen the intake to prevent clogging. Other necessities include locating the pump where water flows to it via gravity or installing a check valve and then priming the pump. Follow the manufacturer's directions for installation and operation.

TYPICAL FLOW RATES FOR WATER FEATURES

Pond, small: 40 to 400 gph
Pond, medium: 100 to 1,000 gph
Pond, large: 400 to 4,000 gph
Fountain: 200 to 400 gph. Check the fountain manufacturer's rating.
Statuary, small: 40 to 150 gph
Statuary, medium: 100 to 400 gph
Statuary, large: 300 to 800 gph
Filter, biological: Recirculates 15 to 25 percent of the water volume per hour.
Filter, mechanical: Recirculates 50 percent of the feature's water volume per hour.
Filter, U.V. light: Recirculates 50 percent of the feature's water volume per hour.
Stream: Recirculates 50 to 100 percent of the feature's water volume per hour.
Waterfall: Recirculates 50 to 100 percent of the feature's water volume; 150 gph per inch of spillway width measured at the fall's discharge height.

BOTTOM DRAINS AND BULKHEAD CONNECTORS

Bottom drains and bulkhead connectors are specialized pipe fittings that allow a watertight passageway for water or power lines to go through a pond liner below the water surface.

A bottom drain allows you to let the water flow out the bottom of your water feature by disconnecting the pump and turning a valve. A bulkhead connection is a specialized fitting on the side of a water feature into which you screw a pipe or pipe fitting. Guard against leaks by following manufacturer's directions carefully when installing a bottom drain or a bulkhead connection in your pond.

Bottom drains

Ponds stocked heavily with fish, especially koi, often include one or more bottom drains. A bottom drain made for koi ponds works just as successfully in water gardens, particularly if stocked heavily with fish. Koi keepers regularly replace 10 percent or more of their pond water. Drains make this easier to do. A 3-inch diameter drain is standard. Installing a 4-inch-diameter drainpipe greatly reduces the likelihood of clogging.

Bottom drains include a removable cover that minimizes suction created as the water drains. This helps to prevent small fish and large debris from passing through and clogging the bottom drain. The drains also include watertight fittings that clamp against a flexible liner or a rigid shell liner. Bottom drains also work well in poured concrete ponds.

Swimming pool drains are too fine and quickly become clogged in a fishpond or water-garden environment. Some filter systems are designed to receive water from the pool bottom, thus making a bottom drain necessary for them.

Bulkhead connectors

The bulkhead connector is a short length of flanged, externally threaded pipe equipped with a locknut and a rubber washer for making a watertight seal. The inside of the pipe is either threaded to accept a variety of pipe fittings or smooth for solvent welding of PVC pipe. The diameter of the pipe that runs through the wall of the feature determines what diameter bulkhead connector you need. Passage for electrical power, overflow water, intake water, or recirculated water for a filter, waterfall, stream, UV clarifier, statuary, or fountainhead are among the uses for a bulkhead connector.

Most water features don't include either a bottom drain or a bulkhead connector. The submersible pump that regularly recirculates the water works well to drain the pond for maintenance. Typically, the water and power lines of a water feature (including many koi ponds) run into the pond between the edging material and the top of the liner, whether the liner is flexible, rigid, or concrete. Cutting a flexible liner or a preformed shell may void the manufacturer's guarantee. What's more, cutting a hole in your liner, even for a bottom drain or bulkhead, increases the chance of a leak.

BOTTOM DRAIN AND AUTOMATIC FLOW VALVE INSTALLATION

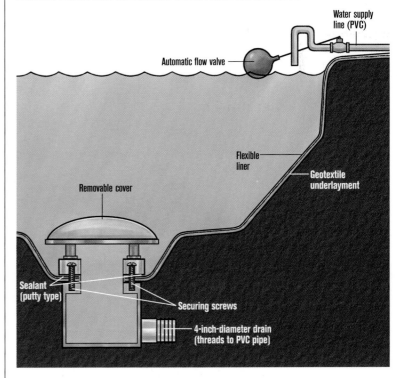

Water supply line (PVC)

Automatic flow valve

Flexible liner

Geotextile underlayment

Removable cover

Sealant (putty type)

Securing screws

4-inch-diameter drain (threads to PVC pipe)

PIPES AND FITTINGS

Today's professionals and amateurs prefer plastic pipe, tubing, fittings, and valves. Their ease of installation, longevity, noncorrosiveness, and nontoxic properties make plastic piping and other supplies ideal for water features.

Flexible vinyl tubing is the least expensive and quickest to install for a water line. If the size of the line you need exceeds a 1-inch inside dimension (ID), use flexible PVC tubing, which is more expensive but easy to install. For 2-inch lines or larger, use rigid PVC pipe. It costs less than flexible PVC and resists being squeezed by traffic or the weight of material that is placed over it.

Use galvanized or bronze supplies if you can't find plastic. Avoid copper, which is costly, deteriorates in acidic soil or water, and requires a plumber for installation.

Flexible tubing and piping

Flexible vinyl tubing has various uses for plumbing water features. Attach one end of the tubing to a pump and attach its other end to the equipment that the pump operates, such as a fountain, waterfall, filter, UV clarifier, or statuary. Or carefully let the line discharge into a waterway basin— the pool of water that overflows at the top of a waterfall. The job might also be more complex. For example, you may attach the line to a UV clarifier and continue with another section of tubing to a filter that empties into a waterfall basin.

Secure a hose clamp around tubing wherever it connects with any equipment to keep it in place and ensure a watertight connection. Match the clamp size to the tubing; use a ½-inch clamp for a ½-inch outside dimension (OD) pipe, for example. *Note:* tubing and piping sizes are usually referred to by their inside diameter (ID).

When connected to a submersible pump, flexible tubing makes it easier to lift the pump for inspection or service. Given a choice, thicker tubing resists kinking and squeezing better than thinner-walled tubing. Avoid bending flexible tubing around a corner, burying it underground, or using it in other ways that would restrict the water flowing through it.

Avoid clear vinyl tubing. The growth of algae is encouraged inside the plastic wherever sunlight can reach, eventually clogging the tubing. Choose black tubing instead; it blocks light and prevents algae accumulation.

Flexible schedule 40 PVC tubing works well for water features. Its flexibility allows the line to run without flow-restricting elbows, yet it's strong enough to resist buckling when covered with soil. Use flexible PVC pipe glue to secure fittings and connections.

Nonkinking corrugated vinyl tubing bends around corners without crimping. Like standard corrugated tubing, it has a wavy exterior, but its smooth interior won't slow water flow. Use clamps with foam strips on the inside that correspond to the ridges and valleys of the corrugated material to create a watertight connection to a pump, filter, clarifier, fountain, or other equipment. This tubing can be buried up to 6 inches deep. Use barbed (also called push-in or compression) fittings, which simply push together to link flexible piping. Then use plastic or stainless steel clamps to secure the connections.

Rigid piping

Rigid PVC pipe is corrosion-resistant, lightweight, and inexpensive. Use schedule 40 PVC pipe to avoid the drawbacks of flexible tubing. Rigid PVC resists compression under the weight of soil, rocks, or foot traffic. In addition, algae doesn't grow inside the opaque white pipe. Choose rigid pipe for runs of 15 to 20 feet or longer, for a water volume of 3,000 gph or more, and for situations where the pipe must be buried underground. Elbows, available in 45- and 90-degree turns, allow a change in the direction of PVC pipe and water flow without significantly reducing the flow.

PIPES

Black vinyl tubing: Clogs and kinks very quickly; it is best used only where short lengths are needed. Black color prevents algae build up.

Rigid PVC: Use schedule 40 pressure-rated pipe and fittings. It is corrosion resistant, lightweight, and inexpensive, but not flexible. Commonly available in white but can be spray-painted black where it's visible underwater.

Corrugated plastic: Extremely flexible, which makes it especially useful for water gardens. Can be expensive and requires barbed fittings with clamps.

Black plastic: Many brands and styles. Semiflexible, inexpensive, and requires barbed fittings and clamps. Good pipe to bury underground. Because it's flexible, it requires fewer elbows.

Metal: Copper or galvanized steel. Can be toxic to some pond life, such as snails and dragonfly larvae. Expensive and not recommended.

Make a rigid water line by cutting lengths of pipe to match the layout you design. (Lengths of PVC pipe cut easily with a hacksaw.) Then fit and glue the pieces together. Use PVC primer and pipe glue to make a watertight connection. Other connection options include threaded fittings (screw) and compression fittings (push). Use Teflon tape on threaded pipe connections to make them watertight. Carefully inspect and flow-test connections to make certain they don't leak.

Tubing and piping size

Pipe diameter is determined by the gph necessary to operate the filter, waterfall, or other features. When buying piping or tubing, increase the diameter to the next larger size when the needed length exceeds 15 feet. A larger diameter reduces water friction against the piping, lessens pressure against the pump, and helps to maintain the desired gph. The size of the piping or tubing you use must match the connection piece (either the discharge or intake) on the pump. For example, buy 1-inch ID tubing if the pump volute (outlet) measures 1-inch OD. If you have 1-inch OD tubing for the pump, use a reducer fitting to connect the pump and tubing. In the case of a pump that takes a 1-inch PVC pipe that would be more than 15 feet long, use 1¼-inch-diameter piping. Use a reducer connection to make the larger pipe compatible with the pump volume.

Assorted fittings

Fittings allow you to regulate, direct, and secure the flow of water through the piping or tubing. Flexible tubing or a hand-tight PVC union makes pump removal quick and easy. If the pump has a threaded female socket and you want to connect it to vinyl tubing, use a polyethylene barb fitting and clamp to do the job. Use standard-socket PVC fittings for PVC pipe and tubing.

■ **Ball valve:** A fast on-off valve, this water-flow regulator operates with a quarter turn of the handle to stop or start the water stream. Inside is a ball with a hole in it. When the hole is aligned with the pipe, water flows through it. When rotated perpendicular to the water flow, the ball blocks the water.

■ **Gate valve:** Use a gate valve to make minor flow adjustments. Turning the handle raises or lowers a barrier (the gate). When it is raised, water flows freely. When

lowered completely, it stops the water flow. You can open or close the gate to any height to adjust water flow.

■ **Knife valve:** Knife valves, also called slide valves, are often used to control water flow to drain lines, filters, and skimmers. Pulling up or pushing down on the handle rapidly shuts off the water for servicing these components of the water feature.

■ **Three-way, or diverter, valve:** This water flow regulator has one inlet and two outlets. Changes in the valve-handle position alter the balance of flow between the two outlets. Use it when one pump is operating two features, such as a filter and a fountain.

■ **Check valve:** Check valves permit water to pass in one direction but stop it if it starts to move the opposite way. Install a check valve on the line between the water and a nonsubmersible pump not fed by gravity. Otherwise, when the pump stops, air gets into the line, and the pump loses its prime.

■ **Globe valve:** A globe valve is too restrictive to use on a water feature because it requires pressure far higher than 40 to 60 pounds per square inch.

■ **Hose clamp:** A hose clamp holds flexible tubing securely to a pump or feature.

■ **Hose restrictor clamp:** A restrictor clamp tightens on flexible tubing to reduce water flow and secure a connection.

■ **Bulkhead connector (Flanged tank adapter):** A bulkhead connector enables a water line to pass out of the feature below the water's surface while preventing the feature from leaking where the lines penetrate the wall.

■ **T-fittings and Y-fittings:** These divide a stream of water into two lines.

■ **Elbows:** Elbows make 45- and 90-degree turns in rigid or flexible pipelines.

■ **Adapters:** Various kinds of adapters make it possible to join rigid pipe to flexible tubing. Socket weld PVC fittings to male/female threaded connections.

■ **Reducer:** A reducer provides a different diameter at each end to connect piping of differing diameters.

■ **Automatic flow valve:** Automatic flow valves ensure that, despite evaporation, the water in a pond, stream, or other feature remains at the desired level. It works like the float valve in a toilet. When working properly, the automatic flow valve could mask a leak that might develop in the pond. If the flow valve malfunctions, the feature may overflow with chlorinated tap water, killing the aquatic life in the pond. If it fails to add water while you're away, the water depth could become dangerously low, harming aquatic life and equipment.

SKIMMERS AND UV CLARIFIERS

A skimmer prevents problems associated with leaves and other debris that fall into your water feature and present a hazard to your fish. As leaves decay and sink, they consume oxygen and produce toxic gases that escape harmlessly into the atmosphere. This isn't a problem until winter, when ice forms on the pond, trapping the gases and killing the fish.

A skimmer removes floating matter before it decays and sinks. It helps maintain water quality by increasing the oxygen level as the skimmed water splashes back into the pond.

How a skimmer works

The skimmer functions as a mechanical filter that sits at the edge of a water feature. A lid on the skimmer top allows access for frequent (at least weekly) cleaning. The top of the skimmer typically sits about 1½ inches above the surface of the pond. If the water level in your feature drops too low, the skimmer runs but does not filter, sucking air instead of water.

Netting within the skimmer traps debris. A pump inside the device works constantly to draw the water into it. Water from the skimmer is then pumped to a filter, waterfall, or other location to recirculate back into the pond.

A skimmer works best when installed downwind, allowing prevailing winds to direct leaves and other floating material toward the skimmer. Recirculated water should re-enter the pond at the opposite side from the skimmer.

You can increase the skimmer's efficiency by locating it opposite the waterfall or stream, as the steady current of water

▲ Netting in this skimmer filters floating debris from the water before it can sink to the bottom and decay. Check it regularly to release any plants, fish, or other aquatic life that may also be pulled in.

entering the pond propels floating debris toward the skimmer.

There are some negatives to using a skimmer. It only recirculates surface water, leaving deeper water unfiltered. While collecting unwanted floating debris, the skimmer may also draw in floating plants. In addition, it sucks in small fish and traps frogs and tadpoles. Check it daily and rescue any trapped pond denizens.

A skimmer requires extra planning to conceal it and extra plumbing to move water from it to the far side of the feature. You will have to incorporate equipment

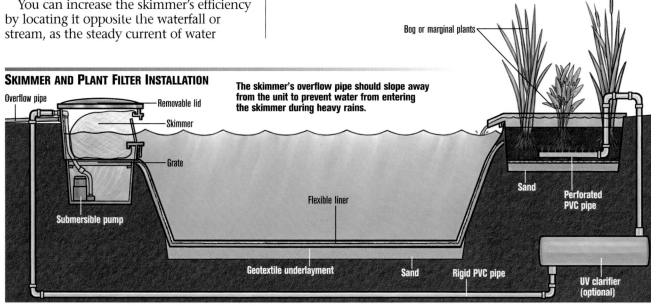

SKIMMER AND PLANT FILTER INSTALLATION

The skimmer's overflow pipe should slope away from the unit to prevent water from entering the skimmer during heavy rains.

Overflow pipe
Removable lid
Skimmer
Grate
Submersible pump
Flexible liner
Geotextile underlayment
Sand
Rigid PVC pipe
Bog or marginal plants
Sand
Perforated PVC pipe
UV clarifier (optional)

such as a filter or fountain along the same plumbing path to increase efficiency. A skimmer may also increase installation investment and adds to operating expense.

If desired, include an automatic flow valve with a pond skimmer to help maintain the appropriate water level.

UV clarifier

If you are looking for a sure way to avoid green water due to algae, you will find it with a UV clarifier. Also known as a UV sterilizer, this device kills suspended algae (planktonic algae), bacteria, and other microorganisms as they flow through the clarifier. A UV clarifier also kills fungi and some parasites that attack goldfish and koi.

A clarifier kills beneficial organisms only if they get into the UV chamber. It won't affect the beneficial bacteria that colonize inside the biofilter and on the sides and bottom of the pond. Aquatic plants should be included in a plan that uses a UV clarifier. Otherwise, you will end up with clear water that is full of nitrites, which can be detrimental to fish.

How a UV clarifier works

A UV clarifier consists of an ultraviolet bulb inside a quartz-glass tube and PVC housing. A pump forces water through a pipe to the UV unit. The water is irradiated as it passes between the inside of the housing and the outside of the glass tube. (The light breaks down algae.) The water then returns to the pond directly or via a biofilter, waterfall, stream, fountain, piped statuary, or bog.

UV clarifiers are labeled according to their wattage, maximum gph, and recommended pond size range. Their strength varies. If the maximum flow rate for the UV clarifier is exceeded, algae will move past the UV light too quickly to be killed. Buy a clarifier with a maximum gph capacity that exceeds the gph of the pump that powers water to it. A higher wattage means that the unit can successfully handle a greater gph.

Because clarifiers kill bacteria, remember to unplug the UV unit when adding beneficial bacteria to a biofilter or directly into the pond. Resume operating it when you want to rid the water of suspended algae. A UV lightbulb is good for a single season, so replace it each spring. Even if the light continues to burn for a new season, its spectrum will no longer be effective.

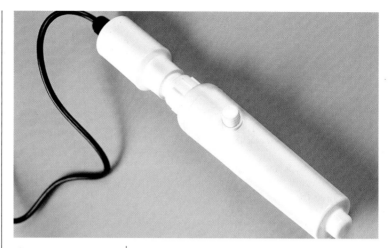

▲ An ultraviolet (UV) clarifier kills suspended algae, bacteria, some fungi, and some parasites that kill fish. It will not harm beneficial bacteria outside the UV chamber.

Magnetic algae controller

This device works to rid the pond of filamentous algae, the kind that adheres to the walls and bottom of the pond, as well as to objects within the pond. A magnetic algae controller also reduces the lime buildup on the quartz tube of a UV clarifier, which improves its effectiveness. The device works in ponds only when the pH is 7.5 or lower. Filamentous algae require the presence of carbon ions to adhere to pond surfaces. Magnets in the unit alter the nature of the ions so that the algae cannot adhere to pond surfaces. Water passes through the unit with no external power required.

An alternate type requires 120-volt standard household power that is reduced to 12 volts by a step-down transformer. Circulated water passes through piping outside the water feature. Electromagnetic units clamped onto the piping modify the carbon ions.

UV CLARIFIER

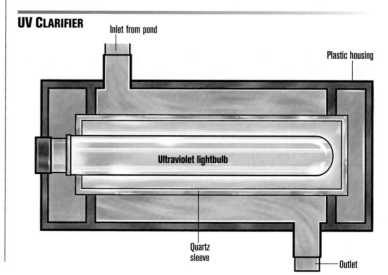

Inlet from pond

Plastic housing

Ultraviolet lightbulb

Quartz sleeve

Outlet

FILTERS

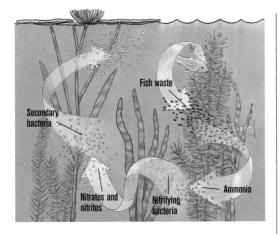

The nitrogen cycle

The most often asked question about water gardening is how to keep the pond water from turning green. The short answer is to minimize the number and size of fish in the water feature and to maximize the number of plants. A basic understanding that fish waste stimulates algae growth will help you to better manage your pond water.

The healthy balance of life in your water feature depends on a phenomenon called the nitrogen cycle. This scientific process of nature is as fundamental to aquatic life as photosynthesis is to plants. Successful pond owners understand how to harness the cycle for their benefit. Ignoring it leads to toxic water with dead fish and scavengers.

▲ **Lava rocks are used for biological filtration. Contained in a drawstring bag, they are easily removed from the waterfall housing for cleaning.**

Basically here's how the nitrogen cycle works: Fish eat food they find in the water, digest it, and later excrete it as waste. This waste matter contains nitrogen in the form of ammonia (NH_3). Uneaten fish food and other organic matter (material from plants or animals) likewise contribute nitrogen in the form of ammonia. If left unchecked, the ammonia becomes deadly to fish and scavengers living in the water.

Beneficial nitrifying bacteria

As ammonia accumulates in the water, beneficial nitrifying bacteria and enzymes break ammonia down into nitrite. These nitrifiers cling to surface areas all around the pond. They reach significant numbers about the same time the mosslike green algae become noticeable on the sides of the pond. Nitrifying bacteria begin their helpful work as the water temperature rises to 50°F and warmer in spring. They slow down in fall as days grow shorter and the water temperature drops below 50°F.

Nitrifying bacteria and enzymes that thrive on nitrite will oxidize nitrite into nitrate, a form of nitrogen generally benign to pond creatures and beneficial to plants. Plants take up the nitrate. Fish and scavengers nibble on the greenery and return nitrogen to the water, completing the nitrogen cycle.

Ammonia

Released into clear, fresh water, healthy fish sometimes lose their appetite and die for no apparent reason. A water test may reveal ammonia in excess of a level safe for fish. That's because during the first four to six

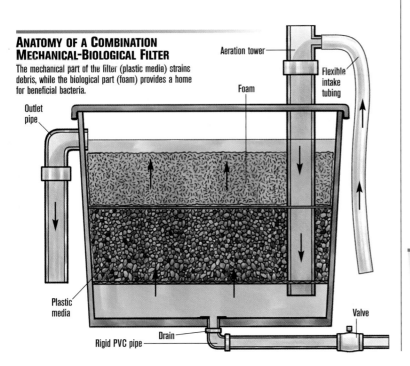

ANATOMY OF A COMBINATION MECHANICAL-BIOLOGICAL FILTER

The mechanical part of the filter (plastic media) strains debris, while the biological part (foam) provides a home for beneficial bacteria.

Outlet pipe

Aeration tower

Flexible intake tubing

Foam

Plastic media

Drain

Rigid PVC pipe

Valve

weeks of a pond's life, the colony of beneficial bacteria is developing and not yet able to handle the load of fish. You can prevent fish kills by seeding the water with additional beneficial bacteria. You can also add only a few fish at the beginning so that the ammonia level doesn't rise faster than the increasing bacteria population can handle.

Remember that fish food, eaten and uneaten alike, contains nitrogen. The more food you put into the water, the more nitrate results. Algae thrive on nitrate. Unless the water feature grows a sufficient quantity of efficient nitrate users, the algae grow out of control. Limiting fish food amounts will reduce the intensity of green water that results from nitrate oversupply.

Stop feeding fish when the water temperature drops below 50°F. At this point, the beneficial nitrifying bacteria slow down from their summertime work. As the lower temperatures slow down the decay of organic matter, the release of toxic ammonia also slows. Overfeeding fish, however, promotes deadly ammonia levels. It's best to allow the pond to reach a natural balance or employ extra help from a biological filter.

People mistakenly believe all green water is bad, but fish thrive in healthy water containing algae. Algae is excessive and needs controlling when you can't see your hand 12 inches beneath the water's surface.

Mechanical filtration

When pond water becomes cloudy, filtration offers a solution. Mechanical filtration forces pond water through porous media (usually filter pads) that catch larger particles. Most mechanical filters sit on the bottom of the water feature, but some work outside the pond.

Capacity

Do not skimp on the capacity of your mechanical filter. To do so simply wastes money. The pump for a mechanical filter should recirculate the feature's water volume at least once every two hours. A 1,000-gallon water feature needs a pump that can recirculate at least 500 gph through the mechanical filter. Better yet, select a unit designed to function at a slightly higher capacity than you need.

If you choose a mechanical pond filter, make sure it's designed to handle the capacity of your water feature. If you

▲ A net bag inside a skimmer filters mechanically by trapping floating debris. Clean it frequently for greatest efficiency.

buy a unit with too little capacity or if you fail to clean it regularly, it will be useless. Swimming pool filters become clogged within hours of filtering pond water because they're designed for use with algae-killing chemicals.

The advantages of mechanical filters include their modest cost, ease of setup, and simple maintenance. Disadvantages include frequency of cleaning and lack of ability to eliminate algae.

BUBBLE-WASHED BEAD FILTER

A bead filter clarifies water by trapping debris. It also works as a biofilter: The beads provide a place for beneficial bacteria to flourish.

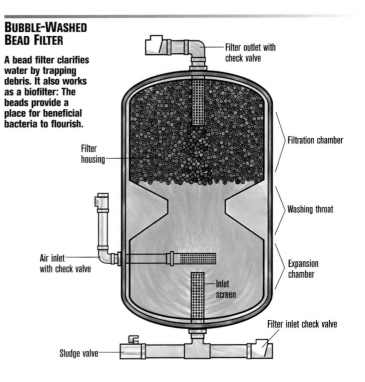

Filter outlet with check valve

Filtration chamber

Filter housing

Washing throat

Air inlet with check valve

Expansion chamber

Inlet screen

Filter inlet check valve

Sludge valve

Filters with an added pump

Most mechanical filters come without a built-in pump. If the filter doesn't have its own pump, connect one that's appropriate for the size of the water feature.

Use a pump (with a minimum gph of half the feature's water volume) that can be connected to the filter using flexible vinyl tubing. Remove the pump's screen or prefilter unit, which covers the intake (where water is drawn into the pump) and is designed to prevent clogging of the pump by keeping out leaves, twigs, and such. Then attach the filter to the pump's intake. Be sure to leave the pump intact. Disassembling it could void the warranty.

Filters with a built-in pump

Mechanical filter units sometimes include recirculating pumps. Easy-to-install kits are sold with filters and pumps sized appropriately to handle the volume of water for various sized ponds. The pump discharges the filtered water either directly into the pond or into flexible tubing to power a waterfall or decorative fountain.

Some mechanical filters operate outside the pond, making cleaning easier. In this case, the water goes first to the pump, which forces the water through tubing to the external mechanical filter. The newly filtered water then flows under pressure to a waterfall or stream or directly into the pond. Before starting this type of filtration system, attach tubing to the pump's discharge and run it to the intake of the filter unit. Then run tubing from the filter outlet to flow into the pond.

The resistance of the filter reduces the volume of water that the pump recirculates.

If for any reason the pump's gph drops too low, the filter's effectiveness is reduced. By the same token, if a filter becomes clogged and a pump's intake is restricted, the pump could become damaged and fail to work.

Recirculate half the water in the pond once per hour or all the water once every two hours. If the pump powers a waterfall 3 feet above the water surface directly above it, the pump should be rated to recirculate at least half the pond water once per hour at the 3-foot head.

Filter maintenance

Mechanical filters usually work out of sight, on the pond bottom. But placing the filter in an easy-to-reach location saves time and effort for the busy owner. If the pond is so deep its bottom cannot easily be reached, consider making a platform for the filter using clean bricks or flat rocks.

You will soon learn to recognize when the filter needs cleaning. Reduced water flow indicates that the filter is clogged with debris. Clean the filter daily during warm summer periods. Be sure that clamps hold the tubing tightly to the filter unit and the pump. Efficiency is lost when water leaks at these points, whether the pump is located inside or outside the pond.

Biological filtration

Biological filtration occurs in water features where plants and naturally occurring bacteria maintain water quality without supplemental filtration. Biofilters work to make water clear and healthy for fish. They work partly as mechanical filters, trapping suspended debris from pond water. In addition, nitrifying bacteria and enzymes inside the biofilter remove ammonia and nitrites from the water.

Various biofilters are popular among koi hobbyists and ornamental-fish dealers. Generally, biofilters are efficient and easy to clean. Every month or two, rinse off one-fourth to one-third of the elements (more than that interferes with the effectiveness of the nitrifying bacteria). Disadvantages of biofilters include their initial cost, complicated installation, and bulk (which makes them difficult to conceal).

■ **How biofilters work:** Filter manufacturers search for ways to maximize the number of nitrifying bacteria and enzymes in a filter unit. These beneficial microscopic creatures spend their lives clinging to any stationary aquatic surface. Filter designers employ

▼ **A skimmer pump recirculates filtered water back to the waterfall, which also helps maintain adequate oxygen.**

elements with as much surface area as possible, such as gravel, volcanic rock, and many imaginative configurations of plastic.

Although the bacteria require oxygen to function, water typically comes into the biofilter from near the bottom of the pond where oxygen levels are low. To remedy this deficiency, better-quality biofilters aerate the water before it reaches the nitrifying bacteria. Aeration yields a more dense population of bacteria, which in turn allows a more space-efficient housing for the filter.

Some biofilters include a space for aquatic plants that absorb nitrogen from nitrates and nitrites. When planted, the filter robs algae of the nutrients they need to thrive, thus enhancing water quality.

Use a water test kit to measure the ammonia or nitrite levels. A biological filter is needed if these test too high. A high reading results from having a greater fish population than can be handled by the nitrifying bacteria and enzymes naturally found in the pond.

■ **Aboveground biological filters:** Most biofilters are designed to operate above the ground outside the pond. The pump sends pond water up to the aboveground filter unit. It is aerated before it flows through the mechanical, debris-removal section. Then it flows through the high-surface section housing the concentrated nitrifying bacteria and enzyme colonies that detoxify the water. In some units, the water passes a final sector of aquatic plants where nutrient removal reduces algae growth. Purified water flows out of the unit via gravity.

■ **In-ground biological filters:** Large ponds, especially koi ponds, frequently utilize in-ground biofilters. Often made of high-density polyethylene, they typically feature round chambers and conical bottoms. A typical unit sits in the ground with its top slightly above water level. An external pump draws water through piping from the pond's bottom drain. At the same time, the pump pulls filtered water from the biofilter.

Easy-to-clean, pressurized biofilters are available for any size pond. These small, in-ground units are accessible and easy to hide with imitation (fiberglass) rocks.

■ **Pressurized biological filters:** Also known as bead filters, these units operate within a pressurized housing. A high-pressure pump draws water from the pond, usually through bottom drains. A pressurized vortex at the pump's intake removes heavy suspended matter from the water. The pump forces the pond water into the filter,

▲ A pump housed below a filter pulls water from the pond through a skimmer net and the filter before returning the water to the pond through a series of waterfalls.

where nitrifying bacteria and enzymes flourish on beads designed with high surface area. The filtration media collect suspended matter in the spaces between the beads. The slow water flow over the huge surface area provided by the beads allows excellent colonization of the bacteria and enzymes. Purified water forced out of the pressurized filter housing then goes to a waterfall or pond.

A pressure gauge on the intake valve indicates when the filter needs cleaning. A decrease in the volume of water coming out of the filter also indicates that the unit needs cleaning. Back flushing for a few minutes does the job. The best units include a propeller to loosen the beads, which sometimes become impacted.

Plant filters

Plant filters make the nitrogen cycle work to your advantage through a simple concept: Pond water filters through an aquatic plant bed, allowing plants to do the work. If you want to make a plant filter, such as a bog, include it as part of the pond construction. Ask at a garden center about plants best suited for this purpose.

■ **How plant filters work:** Nitrifying bacteria and enzymes colonize the plant filter's gravel bed. Gravel serves as a mechanical filter that removes debris. Bacteria and enzymes reduce ammonia in the water to nitrite and then to nitrate. Water-loving marginal or bog plants flourish in the shallow, nitrate-rich water. Most of the suspended matter carried in by the water disintegrates. The gravel filter bed is big enough to function for years without becoming clogged.

ELECTRICAL POWER

You can successfully operate an ecologically balanced water feature without using electrical power. But most water feature owners prefer to add the visual, aural, and biological benefits that moving, splashing, pump-powered water provides. Other pond accessories require electricity as well. Outdoor lighting enables homeowners to view their gardens in the evening. Fishkeepers in cold regions rely on deicers to safeguard their prized fish during winter.

Solar energy or batteries can power pumps and lights. But solar-powered pumps don't work on cloudy days and at night. A submersible pump quickly consumes the energy stored in a battery. Standard household 120-volt alternating current supplies most of the power for today's water features and their accessories. Most outdoor lighting systems use 120-volt or 12-volt power.

Before starting any electrical installation, learn about your local electrical code from your city or county inspector (department of building inspection). Also check the National Electric Code (NEC), which gives minimum standards for outdoor wiring.

Local codes may have specific rules, depending on climate and soil conditions. For example, your local code may require underground power lines to be encased in conduit buried at a certain depth.

Safety first

Low-voltage systems are easy and safe to install. The potential danger of 120-volt power, however, requires strict attention to safety. Working on electrical lines can be life-threatening if you're not extremely careful, especially around water or moisture. Be certain power is turned off and double-check it with a voltage meter. If you're not completely comfortable about doing electrical work, hire an electrician.

For safety's sake, install a ground fault circuit interrupter in each electrical outlet when you plan to use electricity in or near water. In homes with modern wiring, you'll commonly find GFCI electrical outlets in kitchens and bathrooms. The GFCI senses any electrical contact with water in addition to current overload. If water contact occurs, the GFCI instantly stops the electrical current. If aboveground pump wiring becomes frayed and water touches the power wire, the electricity is cut off. Installing a GFCI requires professional-level skills. A less-expensive alternative would be to install a GFCI near the water feature.

Determine the electrical load needed to operate your planned water feature and all

WATER GARDEN ELECTRICAL SETUP

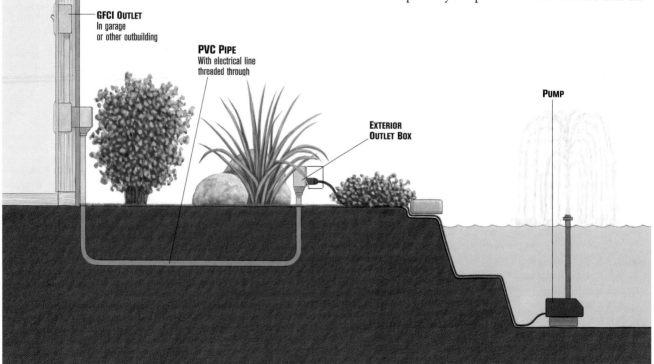

GFCI OUTLET
In garage
or other outbuilding

PVC PIPE
With electrical line
threaded through

EXTERIOR
OUTLET BOX

PUMP

of its components. Pumps and other devices are labeled by the manufacturer according to number of watts or amps. Compare the needed power requirements with the number of amps or watts a circuit can handle. Residential circuit breakers handle 15 or 20 amps per circuit for 1,800 watts to 2,400 watts. Figure amps (current) × volts (potential) = watts (power). For most residential water features, a single 20-amp circuit suffices. If your watts are expected to exceed 2,400, and you need 20 amps or more, install a second circuit to your breaker box. A large nonsubmersible pump might require a 220-volt circuit, which calls for its own dedicated power line from the circuit breaker. Leave such an installation to a licensed electrician.

Electrical line installation

Remember to call your local phone, gas, cable, and electricity providers and ask them to locate and mark all underground utility lines on your property before you dig. When laying new electrical lines underground, avoid traversing any area with a septic system, paving, a deck, a patio, or an outbuilding.

Run the power line through a PVC schedule 40 pipe buried at least 18 inches deep. At this depth, the line is less likely to be damaged by digging near it. Consider installing an electrical switch in the house or on a porch with a waterproof outdoor switch to control the lights or other equipment for your water feature.

Installing a power box or outlet

Ensure the safe and proper installation of a weatherproof GFCI-protected power outlet or a separate box (metal or plastic) by following local building codes. These may specify its location in relation to the water feature as well as the appropriate choice of materials. In addition, determine where the pump and other electrical equipment will be located. Their power cords should reach the GFCI outlet without the use of extension cords.

Set the power box or outlet on short lengths of galvanized pipe by screwing the pipes into openings at the bottom of the box or outlet and securing each with a bushing. Dig a trench as deep as code requires from your home's nearest power box to the location of the new outdoor box or outlet. Run the power line from

▲ Where power and fixture wires join, a cover allows access while enclosing the junction, keeping it watertight.

the breaker panel of your home through rigid metal or schedule 40 PVC pipe and into the outlet or box. For long-term support and stability, attach the pipes to a 2×6 pressure-treated post with metal brackets. Prepare an 18-inch-deep hole for the support post; then pour concrete into the hole around the post. Install a deep box-type outlet cover to shelter the power cords when they are plugged in to avoid an inadvertent tripping of the circuit by rain, dew, or sprinklers.

LIGHTING

You can create amazing effects with water-feature lighting—make a waterfall glow at night, illuminate an entire pond from within, highlight an attractive statue, or heighten the reflection of an overhanging tree.

Water-garden lights are available for installation either in or out of the water. All types, however, should be connected to a GFCI outlet for safety. Those used in the water should be made specifically for underwater use.

Before you shop for water garden lights, experiment with different effects from a powerful flashlight or a spotlight on an extension cord (never place either in the water). Don't get carried away with an effect that detracts from the main feature. Use restraint and subtlety to achieve understated elegance.

There are several types of in-water lights. Each creates its own special effect, depending on how you position it (see the photos on this page and page 55 for examples). Most designs call for lights that have dark, subdued casings so they are hidden by water or plants. Stainless steel or white casings can be obtrusive, especially during daytime.

Waterfall lights and other types of directed lights, either in white or colors,

▲ **Colorful floating water lily lights add sparkle to the water garden during evening hours.**

◀ **Draw attention to a special water feature or favorite tree with a spotlight hidden among edging rocks.**

add drama to water spray. Some also come equipped with transparent wheels of several colors. For best natural effect, colored light should be used sparingly.

Many lighting kits include built-in timers that allow you to turn the lights on and off automatically. You can also install an independent timer in the lighting setup. Timers not only save you the trouble of regulating the lights daily, but also save energy costs.

Lighting extends your enjoyment of a water feature. You might choose bright, high-intensity halogen lights that virtually turn night into day. You may prefer subtle, low-voltage lighting that adds mystery and romance to the evening garden. Solar lights eliminate the need for electrical installation. A hanging light or a wall light draws attention to an otherwise unseen feature near your house. Strategically placed spotlights, angled to shine high or low, highlight special features. Soft pathway lights help guide visitors around an area. Edge the perimeter of a water feature with gentle highlights that reflect the water's surface and dance on the ripples of a waterfall. Use small, brightly colored floating lights on the water's surface to create a festive atmosphere for parties.

Illuminate a waterfall with an inner glow or add drama to a pond using submersible

lighting. Submersible lights come with their own platform so that they can be moved about the pond floor to satisfy changing requirements. They function best when the water is clear. Light dissipates in murky water, accentuating the fact that the pond is not clear.

After measuring and carefully planning what you want to accomplish with lights, you have two choices for powering them: low-voltage (12-volt) or line-voltage (120-volt) outdoor lighting. Remember, any lighting placed in or near the water feature should be connected to a GFCI outlet.

▲ Point spotlights toward the water in the direction of the viewer. Be sure they are not directly aimed toward a neighbor's home.

▼ Submersible lights can be directed up to illuminate a waterfall for nighttime viewing.

▲ Pathway lights keep visitors safely on land and softly highlight the contours of a water feature.

EDGING

Edging materials add the finishing touch to a pond, stream, or waterfall. Enhance the aesthetic appeal of a natural-looking feature by concealing the exposed edges of the liner. Use edging to protect the liner from the harsh effects of the sun. A slightly raised edge also protects the pond from water runoff from the surrounding landscape.

Consider the look and function of your water feature when choosing edging material. Formal pond designs usually have geometric shapes, a level capstone, and one type of edging. Informal ponds are often irregularly shaped and include more than one type of edging. Edging gives birds and other wildlife access to your pond or stream. Even if you don't anticipate people standing near the water, construct the edging with safety in mind. Ensure the edging can withstand your weight combined with that of a visitor or two.

Edging a preformed water feature is more difficult than concealing a flexible liner. Unless the surrounding area is paved, take extra steps to disguise the rim. If you use heavy rocks or pavers as edging, support them with a foundation of concrete blocks or a layer of crushed stone topped with sand buried around the perimeter of the liner to support the lip. Make sure that the stones overhang the edge by 2 inches, or at least enough to conceal the lip.

▲ A skillful design surrounded by drystack stone artfully blends an aboveground pool into the landscape.

▼ Stacked rocks of various sizes disguise the edge of a liner and create a realistic look for a water feature. Flat rocks, adequately secured, provide places to stand or step across.

Natural-looking ponds and streams

A concrete edge along a stream will not look natural. Instead, consider hiding the liner edge under a ledge of soil topped with a combination of rocks and plants for the most natural look. Placing large, flat-topped rocks at strategic points along the stream provides steps as well as seating. A grouping of various-sized rocks looks natural. If you have a large pond with a flexible liner, try creating a gently sloping pebble beach along one side. This allows wildlife to wade and bathe or, as raccoons do, wash their food in the shallow water.

■ **Rock and stone:** These popular edging materials provide a look that's as natural as the ponds and streams they border. Choose rocks indigenous to your area. If there are no rocks in the native landscape, buy rocks that blend naturally with the local terrain. Granite and slate are hard and long-lasting. Their exposed strata, or layers, add a rugged beauty to the water's edge. They're well-suited to waterfalls because running water won't wear away the stone. Sedimentary rocks, including sandstone and limestone, are readily available and reasonably priced edging materials. These soft rocks will deteriorate over time.

Avoid rocks that present a hazard to pond inhabitants. Fresh-cut limestone can make the pond water toxic to fish, and rainwater leaches the toxins into the pond even when the rocks are set beyond the water level. Stabilize rocks or stones with mortar and reinforcing materials so that overhanging rocks are less likely to fall into the water or shift under the weight of a visitor. One or more large boulders at the pond's edge create a dramatic effect but need extra concrete reinforcement to support their weight. To create a visual transition, surround boulders with several smaller rocks of the same type. Also consider partially submerging some stones in the water.

Plants: Create a naturally soft, pleasing look by alternating plants between areas of rocks. Avoid encircling the water feature with a solid necklace of rocks. Low-growing evergreens work well along the perimeter of most water features. Add plants after completing pond construction and installing edging.

Turf: Grass growing to the edge of the water feature looks neat and natural. It provides a good surface on which to reach the water to do maintenance or to observe fish. Skim grass clippings out of the water after mowing. Algae growth results as the high nitrogen in grass disturbs the ecological balance of the pond. Avoid using lawn chemicals, such as herbicides and fertilizers, which might run into your pond or stream when it rains and harm the pond life.

Formal ponds

Cut stone, decorative tiles, cast concrete pieces, or bricks typically edge formal water gardens. Arrange them in the geometric pattern of your choice or combine several types for an unusual, decorative look. Experiment by combining stones and colors at the water's edge to make sure you will be happy with the results. If your pond has curved edges, consider using retaining-wall blocks with a trapezoidal shape.

Set edging on a concrete collar or a 3-inch-deep bed of leveled crushed stone. Use mortar to hold the stone, tile, or block in place. Bricks, mortar, and some rocks could raise the pH level of the water and possibly harm fish. Test the water regularly and adjust the pH level accordingly.

▼ After you've edged it with bricks and concrete pavers, complete a pond's natural surroundings with a variety of plants.

▲ Untreated wood decking provides a contemplative spot right at the water's edge.

Wood edging and decking

Wood looks handsome when combined with turf and other edging materials or used as the surface for a deck or walkway. However, do not use treated lumber. It can leach chemicals into a water feature and pose a toxic threat to plants and fish. Use rot-resistant woods, such as cedar or redwood, or manufactured composite woods. Before using redwood, let it age for a year until it turns gray. Fresh redwood contains tannins toxic to aquatic life. If you like the look of wood edging, consider setting treated timbers, cut pier-style and positioned upright, in a bed of concrete around the pool's perimeter. Alternatively, build a deck over the edge of the water or along the perimeter of the water feature. An overhanging deck offers a place to sit, feed fish, or just watch the water.

INSTALLING A WATER FEATURE

Building a water garden is not a particularly difficult task, even for a beginner. All you need are a few simple tools. With two exceptions—electrical work and large excavations—you probably won't need to hire an outside contractor. For small jobs with simple electrical work, you may be able to wire the pond yourself, if such work is allowed in your community.

Excavation of even a small installation is often the most taxing part. The key to whether it's fun or frustrating lies in how much you can do by yourself without overdoing it. For an extensive project, you will probably be better served to hire someone with a backhoe to do the work (or to rent one, if you have the skill to operate it.)

▼ **Use a carpenter's level resting on a long, straight board to check that the edge of the pool is level along its entire perimeter. If one edge is higher than another, add and tamp soil until the sides are even.**

Water feature installation, like most home improvement projects, is easier to accomplish if you have someone to help. Whether you are installing liner, laying stone, hauling dirt, or just needing a second opinion, a companion greatly speeds up the project.

As you launch into building your water feature, allow ample time for each step. Most homeowners are overly optimistic with their estimate of the time needed to complete a project. Anticipate some complications, trips to the hardware store, and other time-consuming tasks. The installation can be almost as enjoyable as the finished product if you just take your time.

DIGGING

1 Mark the outline of the pond with a garden hose, rope, or sprinkled line of flour, fine soil, or garden lime. Live with the outline for a week or so to discover how well the new feature fits into the landscape and how it will affect traffic patterns.

2 Remove turf. Use it to fill bare spots in the lawn or set it aside in a pile of its own to compost. If you have a large quantity, use it as the base of a berm or a raised bed. Stack it in the spot for the berm and cover it with several inches of topsoil.

3 As you dig, keep the pond edge level. If it is not level, the liner will show. Check by resting a carpenter's level on a straight board laid across the pond. Work all around the pond, checking every shelf and side to be sure they are level.

The most daunting part of creating a large garden pond is the digging. But with some advance planning—and when done properly—digging can be downright fun.

Advance planning

When planning your garden pond, take into consideration how much digging you can do and adjust either the size of the water garden or the amount you do alone. Digging even a small pool is not a job for a person with a history of back pain or heart problems.

■ **Getting help:** If you can't dig it yourself, consider hiring a neighborhood teen or getting friends and relatives to assist. For very large projects, you may want to hire professional help. As a rule, water gardens with a surface area of less than 250 square feet are most economically built by hand. Larger projects are best done with a backhoe, rented or hired.

■ **Time:** Allow ample time for digging, considering both pool size and soil type. An 18-inch-deep, 3×5-foot pool in sandy soil may take only an hour or so, while a 24-inch-deep, 6×10-foot pool in clay can take a day or more. Pace yourself. Even if you're in good physical shape, divide larger projects into one-hour increments with a half-hour rest between so you don't strain your back.

■ **Tools:** Make sure your tools are in excellent condition and well-suited to the task. Start with a sharp spade with a pointed blade. You'll also need a cart or wheelbarrow for hauling dirt and possibly a truck to haul away soil.

It's best to dig when the soil is moist but not wet. That allows the spade to cut through the soil neatly, and the soil isn't overly heavy. If the weather has been dry, you can moisten the top foot or so of soil by soaking it with water from a hose. Let the soil drain before you start digging.

Digging in

Start by marking the site with a garden hose, rope, or garden lime. Then fine-tune the outline with stakes (every foot or so) and twine. Cut along the outline with a spade; then remove the top layer of sod. If you plan to use turf as edging, cut the sod approximately 4 inches in from the outline of the pond. Remove the sod inside the outline and peel back the 4-inch strip. After installing the liner, trim the excess, bury the remaining liner edge, and flip the sod back over it.

HINT

Separate good-quality topsoil, which you can reuse, and poor-quality subsoil, which you should discard, by tossing them into different wheelbarrows or onto different pieces of plastic or tarp.

4 Create a spot to overwinter plants and fish. In cold areas, you'll need a zone in the pool that won't freeze. It should be up to 3 feet deep and as wide as it is deep. Be sure this deep zone isn't in the same spot you want to place a pump or fountain.

5 Dig the shelf for the marginal plants about 8 to 12 inches deep. Position the shelf so that the plants frame your view of the water garden. Then dig a ledge for the edging as deep as the edging material and slightly less wide.

6 Toss the soil into a wheelbarrow or onto a tarp to protect your lawn. If it's in good condition, use it to fill in low spots in the landscape or to build a slope for a waterfall. Otherwise, haul it to a construction site that needs fill dirt.

To edge with stones or other material, dig an outwardly sloping shelf (6 to 8 inches wide by 2 inches deep) for the liner and the edging. The trench should be deep enough for the edging stones to sit flush with the ground or 3 to 4 inches deep for a concrete footing for edges that will get heavy traffic.

With the sod removed, mark the outlines for marginal shelves. Begin digging from the center outward. Dig 2 inches deeper than the pool depth to allow for sand underlayment (less for other materials).

As you dig, angle the sides slightly (about 20 degrees) and keep the pond edges level to prevent the liner from showing. With a small project, you can place a carpenter's level on a straight piece of 2×4 to check all around the pond.

For a large project, put a stake in the center of the pond with its top at the planned water level. Rest one end of a long straight board on the stake and the other end on the edge of the pool. Check the level. Rotate the board a few feet, again noting the level. Repeat until you return to the starting point.

Use the removed sod to patch bare spots in the yard or add it to a compost pile. If the topsoil is in reasonably good condition, add it to the vegetable garden, spread it on flower beds, or create new beds and berms. If you're installing a rigid liner, set aside the soil to backfill around the liner. Put the soil in a wheelbarrow or on a large tarp or piece of plastic to protect the lawn. Discard clay-laden subsoil or use it to build up a slope for a waterfall. Dump larger amounts at a landfill.

PROPER DIGGING TECHNIQUE

Digging your garden pond correctly will save you minor aches and pains as well as possible serious injury.

Wear the proper clothes. A good pair of heavy boots helps you plant your feet, keeps you from slipping, and lets you work more efficiently, reducing fatigue. While digging, be sure to keep a straight back and good posture. Don't stoop or let your shoulders slump. Also keep your knees bent at all times. This distributes weight to your legs. Lift with your legs, not your back.

Work when the soil is reasonably moist—but not wet—to minimize the effort of cutting into the earth without adding much weight to the soil. Scoop up small amounts of soil at a time. Keep loads on the spade reasonably small to prevent strain. Grip the spade close to the blade to give yourself better control.

When carrying soil away from the pond to the place where you'll dump it, walk with your knees slightly bent. Don't stretch out your body to toss the soil in a pile far away; this will overextend your back. As soon as the hole is large enough, step in and work from inside it.

▲ Digging the wrong way

▲ Digging the right way

INSTALLING FLEXIBLE LINER

▲ Smooth the liner into the excavation, creating a few large folds of excess material in order to eliminate most of the smaller ones. Working with one or more friends makes this task easier. Wear only socks or soft-soled shoes to prevent punctures in the liner.

Lay a protective 2-inch base of damp sand on the bottom of the excavation. Use the sand base to fine-tune the gentle bottom slope. On the pond walls, install an underlayment of geotextile fabric, newspapers, or old carpet. Extend the underlayment to cover the sand bottom for extra protection. Set preformed concrete pads in the bottom of the pond to support objects heavier than 200 pounds that will be placed in the pond, such as statuary, boulders, and bridge piers. Cover the concrete pads with carpeting before installing the pond liner. Once the liner is installed, place three or four layers of scrap pond liner on top of the pond liner over the concrete pad. Lower the heavy object slowly and carefully onto the prepared area.

Prior to completing the installation of the protective underlayment, carefully recheck the measurements of the hole using a flexible measuring tape. Measure the length of the excavation by starting at the edge. Lay the tape down the sidewall, across the bottom, and up the opposite sidewall to the edge. Add 2 feet to this measurement to determine the minimum length of the pond liner. Measure the width on a line perpendicular to the length, measuring down the sidewall, across the bottom, and up the opposite sidewall. Add 2 feet to the measured width. Compare the measured results with the dimensions of the pond liner before opening the carton (you may need to exchange the liner for a different size). See page 32 for more details about measuring for a liner.

Unfolding the liner

Carry the liner into the excavation with assistance if needed. Dragging could harm the liner and might pull damaging objects on top of the protective underlayment.

Cold liners, especially those made of PVC, may require an hour in the sun to become pliable. Leaving the liner in place too long—as little as several hours on a hot day—could kill the grass beneath it.

Starting at the center of the pond, unfold the liner outward toward the sides. Center the liner over the excavation. Wear soft-soled shoes or go barefoot when walking on the liner to protect it. The liner will bunch up at the curves and corners. Folds are an inevitable result of forming a two-dimensional piece of material into a three-dimensional shape. Create a few large folds in order to eliminate most of the smaller ones. Let one person pull the liner from the top edge while another person works inside the excavation, making adjustments and ensuring that the liner remains centered in the excavation. Place smooth stones or bricks on the perimeter of the liner to prevent it from blowing into the pond.

Tucking and folding

Informal pools will have random folds along the sides. Rectangular formal pools should have one large fold at each corner. For large folds form each as a large triangle and secure it with double-sided seaming tape. Allow the seaming tape to cure for 24 hours (or as directed) before adding water. Sealing not only makes the fold less obvious but also keeps out debris and prevents small fish from becoming trapped behind the liner.

The time spent folding the pond liner should be minimal, less than 20 minutes for a 10×10-foot pool. Usually, the person most concerned about folds and tucks is the pond owner. Few viewers ever take note of them. If debris falls into the lined pond, sweep the material into a plastic dustpan. When the liner is in place, fill the pond with 2 inches of water before making final adjustments to the liner by smoothing out some of the wrinkles. Finish filling the pond before edging it. After the pond is filled, check for low spots around the edge. If water doesn't cover the liner evenly to the top or spills over the edge in places, lift the liner and add packed sand or packed soil in those places.

If you exercise care during the liner installation, no damage should occur. However, if you do puncture the liner, it is easily repaired with special adhesive tape or other sealants designed for this purpose.

1 Cushion the hole with underlayment. Use moist sand (horizontal surfaces only), old carpet, geotextile fabric made for water gardens, or layers of newspaper. Cover both the bottom and the sides. At corners and curves, cut triangles in the underlayment to fit contours.

2 Position the liner. Drape it loosely in the hole, arranging and pleating as needed. (Two or more people will make this job faster and easier.) Anchor the sides with bricks or stones, taking care not to stretch the liner.

3 Adjust the liner. Add a few inches of water to the pond to settle the liner. Pleat and tuck the liner as necessary to make it fit the contours and corners of the pond.

4 Prepare for edging. Fill the pond with a few more inches of water. Adjust the liner and add more water to just below the edging shelf.

INSTALLING PREFORMED LINER

hoose the largest liner possible that suits your site and your pocketbook. Preformed units appear smaller once installed, filled with water, and edged. If you want to keep koi or goldfish, the pond should be deep enough to accommodate them; if it has plant shelves, they should be wide enough to hold the pots you will use for planting.

After determining where you want to install your pond, carry the preformed unit to the site. Orient the liner, topside up, on the spot where you want to install it. Use a carpenter's level and plumb bob or a weighted string to establish the outer edge of the pond. You can't simply mark the outline of the form's bottom on the ground and start digging. Preformed rigid pond walls slope slightly inward (from top to bottom), making the top perimeter larger than the bottom perimeter. The plumb bob drops straight down from the top perimeter, enabling you to outline the perimeter on the ground directly below it. Mark the perimeter using a rope or a hose. Enlarge the entire perimeter by 2 inches to allow working room within the excavation. The extra space will be filled later with sifted soil or sand. Finalize the outline by marking it with spray paint, flour, or sand.

Excavating the site

The liner must have firm support under the shelves, bottom, and sides in order to be stable and resist buckling. Set aside the preformed pool while you excavate. If the pond has no shelves, dig straight down (or

▲ Use a carpenter's level to make sure the sides are level. Remove the liner to add or remove damp sand as needed, then check again with your level.

at a slight angle no greater than the inward slope of the preformed unit) to the bottom. The depth should match the depth of the pond form plus 2 inches. If the pond includes shelves, measure carefully to make the excavation conform to their depth and width. The shelves need to be supported by soil in order to sustain the weight of water when the pond is filled. Leave room to add 2 inches of damp sand under the shelves once the excavation is complete. Damp sand stays in place, whereas dry sand tends to shift off the edges of shelf areas during installation. If you want the top of the preformed liner to be 1 inch above ground level to protect the pond from surface runoff, then measure and dig out only 1 inch extra. The 2 inches of added sand will put the pond top 1 inch above ground level.

Avoid overdigging the shelf areas. Backfilling an excavated space under a shelf could cause the shelf to settle while the remainder of the pond remains stable. This would make the top uneven and allow water to overflow the edge around the plant shelf.

Decide in advance what to do with the soil removed during excavation. You may use it to build up an area planned for a waterfall or to change the contour of the land somewhere else on your property. Ask friends or neighbors if they need the soil or look for a place wanting clean fill dirt.

Preparing the excavation

Spread 2 inches of damp sand across the bottom of the excavation and on the shelf surfaces. Use a board or the straight edge of

POND WITH A PREFORMED LINER

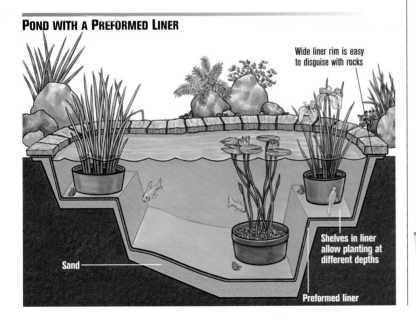

Wide liner rim is easy to disguise with rocks

Shelves in liner allow planting at different depths

Sand

Preformed liner

a garden rake to spread the sand evenly over the entire bottom and the shelves. Place the liner into the excavation. Use a carpenter's level to verify that the pond is level. If it needs leveling, remove the preformed liner and rework the sand. The pond's contact marks on the sand indicate where to remove high sand and where fill-in sand is needed. Continue working the sand until the pond comes within ¼ inch of level.

Perhaps you plan to have a raised pond or one that is partially in the ground and partially above the ground. If it is to be partially in the ground, dig down as already described, but only far enough so that the top of the pond will be at the height desired. Remember to account for the 2 inches of sand added to the excavation. For an aboveground pond, remove the top 2 inches of soil and replace it with sand. Rake and work the sand so that the top of the pond sits level.

Backfilling

Despite being made of rigid fiberglass and high-density polyethylene, preformed ponds have some flexibility. Units built of these materials typically possess sufficient structural integrity to hold water without outside support. But because they are somewhat flexible, they may become distorted when filled if the sidewalls are not supported. Prevent the distortion by filling the space between the sidewalls and the excavation with packed sand or sifted soil as you fill the pond with water. Avoid using vacuum-formed pools, such as children's wading pools, because they easily change shape in undesirable and unpredictable ways. They are also difficult to install and maintain.

As the first few gallons of water spread evenly across the bottom of the liner, it's likely that the form will sit level in the ground. However, the weight of added water might cause a slight shift. As the pond fills, backfill around the form. Adjust the water flow so that the pond fills to roughly the same level at which you are working the sand on the outside of the liner. Periodically check the level in all directions three or more times while the pond is filling with water. If it's out of level by more than ¼ inch, remove the water and soil, make necessary adjustments, and start over. Add the edging to complete the installation.

INSTALLING PREFORMED LINER

1 Before digging, place the prefabricated pool upright where it will be located, then map the outline using a garden hose or rope.

2 Use a carpenter's level to check that the bottom and shelves of the excavation are completely level.

3 Comb the sand with a straight-edged board to ensure that the sand underlayment is smooth.

4 Lift the liner and lower it into the excavation. You may need to remove it several times to make adjustments for a perfect fit.

5 Fill the unit with 4 inches of water. Begin backfilling around it with sand, tamping the sand as you work. Gradually add more water as you backfill, keeping the levels of sand and water comparable.

CONSTRUCTING A CONCRETE POND

Begin with an excavation that allows for a bottom at least 6 inches thick (4 inches in frost-free, earthquake-free areas) plus an additional 4 to 6 inches of gravel. The walls should be equally thick. The top of the concrete should extend 1 inch above the surface of surrounding ground to keep runoff out of the pond.

For large or irregular-shaped ponds, hire a contractor to apply gunite or other sprayed concrete to an excavation lined with reinforced wire mesh. Otherwise, build wood forms that will shape the concrete into the desired design. The walls of the form must be put together carefully because the concrete walls will be an exact impression of the form. Make sure that the tops of the form are level. Walls cannot be altered once they are installed.

▲ **Rebar mesh is placed in the side walls and bottom of concrete ponds for added strength and reinforcement.**

▼ **If your pond is inaccessible to large trucks, you may need to carry the concrete to the site in a wheelbarrow.**

In cold climates, consider making the walls 1 inch to 2 inches thicker at the bottom than at the top and angled slightly outward from bottom to top. The angle allows the walls to withstand the pressure of ice.

The pond bottom

In areas subject to winter freezing, reinforce the bottom and walls with rebar or wire mesh. Add a 6-inch-deep layer of gravel to make a solid base that reduces the risk that the concrete will settle and crack.

When pouring the concrete for the pond bottom, make a saucerlike depression approximately 4 inches deep where you can place the pump when you want to empty the pond. The pond floor should slope toward the depression at the rate of 1 inch per 10 feet of bottom. This eliminates the need to install a drain (and prevents clogged drain problems) in the water garden.

Pouring the pond

For best results, pour the concrete in one day—ideally on a cool, cloudy day. If pouring during hot weather, cover the poured construction with opaque plastic sheeting to allow the concrete to cure slowly. The entire pond should be poured in a continuous process—first the floor, then the walls—to make a seamless form. The pond floor should be carefully smoothed, beginning at one end and working backward toward the opposite end and maintaining a slight slope toward the center, where the drain will sit.

Extra security

Concrete ponds can eventually develop hairline cracks and begin to leak in a decade or so. Postpone the leaking by using a flexible pond liner around the exterior of a concrete pond. Lay a base for the liner with 2 inches of gravel topped with 2 inches of sand. Place underlayment of old carpeting or geotextile fabric over the sand and install the flexible liner over that. Pour the concrete floor over the liner and then pour the walls. After removing the wall forms, wrap the excess liner and underlayment over the exterior and top of the pond walls and backfill the space between the underlayment and the excavation walls with sand or sifted soil.

INSTALLING ABOVE GROUND

Aboveground pools and ponds are good options where digging would be difficult. They're also appealing because they bring the water up close, an especially enjoyable touch near a patio or other sitting area.

Raised water features tend to take longer to build than sunken ponds and usually cost more. However, they're less likely to become cluttered with blowing debris or eroding soil.

Types: Aboveground pools must be built from materials sturdy enough to withstand the outward pressure of water. Raised water features are often made of brick, an excellent material in formal gardens or in landscapes that already contain brick. Another option is concrete block veneered with stucco, brick, tile, or stone. Stacked wood timbers or logs stacked on end in a row are other possibilities. Cut or natural stone is another popular choice.

Height: The height of an aboveground pool can vary from 1 foot to much higher. A completely aboveground pool has an ideal height between 24 and 30 inches, especially if you want visitors to see the fish or sit on the edge.

The pool should be at least 18 inches deep. For a pool that rises above ground less than that height, partially excavate the pool to make it 18 inches deep. Doing this ensures the feature will also be better insulated from the elements.

Footings: A masonry aboveground pool will need a concrete footing around the perimeter of its base. The depth of the footing depends on your climate. It may need to be more than 2 feet deep in northern regions. Check local codes for proper depth. You can pour the footing directly into a trench. In soft soil you may need to build wooden forms for the footing. Either way, make sure the footing is perfectly level from one side to the other.

INSTALLING ABOVE GROUND—RIGID LINER

1 Rigid liner works well for creating an aboveground pond with stone sides.

2 Set each successive course slightly closer to the liner and then backfill.

3 Backfill under the liner lip and conceal the edge with overhanging stones.

Materials: Wooden raised pools are simple to make. Masonry projects require more time and skill. Structures made of wood are most successful when constructed from pressure-treated lumber or aged redwood to prevent rot. The wood should be relatively smooth to prevent ripping the flexible liner during installation.

No matter what material you use for the sides of your raised feature, the pool will need to be underlaid and lined. Rigid liner works well for raised gardens, but flexible liner offers more options for style and shape. Staple the liner to the edges of wooden structures or glue it to them with silicone sealant. In masonry projects, sandwich the liner between the last course of brick and the cap.

INSTALLING ABOVE GROUND—FLEXIBLE LINER

1 Bury the bottom ties for stability. Secure wood ties with threaded steel rods at 8- to 10-inch intervals.

2 Add a 2-inch layer of sand on the bottom. Then cover all surfaces with an underlayment for protection.

3 Position the liner and pleat carefully. Fill the pool halfway. Then staple the liner into place and conceal the edge.

MAKING A BOG

You can make a bog garden as an independent unit or as a part of other water features—a pond, a stream, or a waterfall. The bog can absorb water that overflows from your water feature after heavy rains. Integrating a bog with other features takes only a little extra work to make it function as a plant filter that absorbs pollutants and silt.

In nature, streams and ponds have wet, boggy areas along their edges. In garden settings, a bog imitates a marshy place where plants grow in standing water or wet, spongy ground. Water-loving plants thrive because the soil doesn't dry out. If you have a site large enough, you can construct a freestanding bog, as described here. Another option is to install bog plants in the moist margins of a stream or pond to blend the boundaries of water and land.

Making a bog

Bog garden construction differs from pond construction mainly in depth. Excavate a bog 12 to 16 inches deep with sloping sides, saving the soil to refill the bog later. Spread a 2-inch layer of sand and top it with a piece of flexible liner. If the site is normally moist, no underlayment is necessary. In heavy clay soils you may perforate the bottom of the liner every 3 feet to allow drainage and prevent standing water from becoming foul. Do not perforate the liner in sandy soil.

Build a rim of soil and extend the bog's liner 1 inch above the surrounding ground to keep water from running off. Use rocks, soil, and plants around the perimeter to disguise the liner's edge and give the bog a natural look.

Planting the bog

Many bog plants spread easily, quickly overrunning slower-growing species. Keep this in mind when you create a planting scheme. You need to determine where to locate plants and decide if you will plant in containers. Use plastic nursery pots or water garden baskets to contain invasive plants. Otherwise, plant directly in the soil. Saturate the soil, using a leaky hose laid on or under the soil surface.

Adding a bog garden

Build a bog adjacent to a lined pond or stream by extending the liner of the water feature into the bog excavation. The boundary between the water feature and the bog must be semipermeable. This allows water to seep into the bog and saturate the soil. Where the two features meet, the soil should be bermed and hard-packed. After you extend the liner over this berm and into the bog, stack rocks or concrete blocks on the bermed area to keep the soil out of the pond but allow water to seep through.

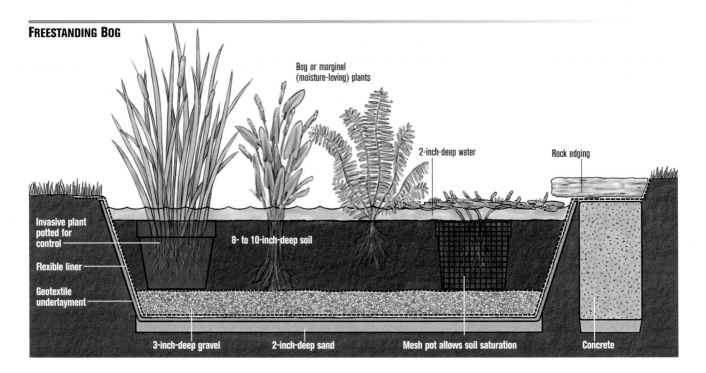

FREESTANDING BOG

Bog or marginal (moisture-loving) plants

2-inch-deep water

Rock edging

Invasive plant potted for control

Flexible liner

Geotextile underlayment

8- to 10-inch-deep soil

3-inch-deep gravel

2-inch-deep sand

Mesh pot allows soil saturation

Concrete

CONSTRUCTING A STREAM

A stream typically runs from a waterfall to a pond. However, it can also function independently or be used with another element such as a bog garden. Design a stream so that it looks like a part of nature. Study the contours of your landscape. If your yard has a slope, it will be easy to turn it into a watercourse.

Consider creating a series of long pools between vertical drops in the stream. Even if your yard is flat, you can create a slope with fill dirt or soil left over from your excavation. A vertical drop of 1 to 2 inches per 10 feet of length provides adequate flow. Pack the soil to stabilize it.

STREAM CONSTRUCTION

1 Mark out the watercourse with stakes or twine. Build up a berm if necessary to create a slope. Then begin digging, creating pools first and spillways next.

2 Install sand or underlayment to prevent tears in the flexible liner. Spread the liner and fold it as needed. Overlap higher sections onto lower ones, check their positions, and seal the seams.

3 Position the pump in the pond at the opposite end from the waterfall or stream. Attach the pump to the piping in the pond and run it up the stream to the outlet.

4 Turn on the pump and check to see how the water flows. Make adjustments by adding or removing soil under the liner.

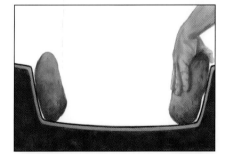

5 Lay a row of rough stones along the stream edges. Use black foam sealant or mortar them to prevent water from flowing under them and being wasted.

6 Disguise the liner edges with pebbles or stones in the streambed. Scatter some among the edging stones too. Avoid gravel, as it tends to collect algae.

7 With the pump running, experiment with the placement of larger stones to see how they affect the water's sounds and movement. Add, subtract, or reposition stones to achieve the desired effect. Trim the liner edges.

INSTALLING A PREFORMED WATERFALL

▲ **This preformed waterfall features three tiers of catch basins. The resin material of which it is made resembles carved stone.**

Preformed waterfalls allow for simple do-it-yourself installation. Some units include a built-in filter. Consult the manufacturer's guidelines for installation and suggested range of gallons per hour (gph). Too much flow can cause water loss and too little flow can cause loss of visual and aural impact.

Fiberglass and foam waterfalls

Choose a waterfall that corresponds with your desired design. Then determine the size of the submerged pump you will need. If the preformed waterfall you choose has a built-in filter, make sure its capacity matches the size of your pond. Select a site for the preformed waterfall and place it there. Observe the setup for several days and try another site if necessary. Excavate the permanent site and make it level from side to side. Tamp the ground to make it more stable. Then cover it with a 2-inch base of sand. Set the preformed unit in place. Make sure the unit overlaps the pond enough to help prevent water loss. Attach the waterfall to the pond liner following the manufacturer's directions.

CROSS SECTION OF INTERLOCKING ISSUING BASIN AND CASCADE WATERFALL UNIT

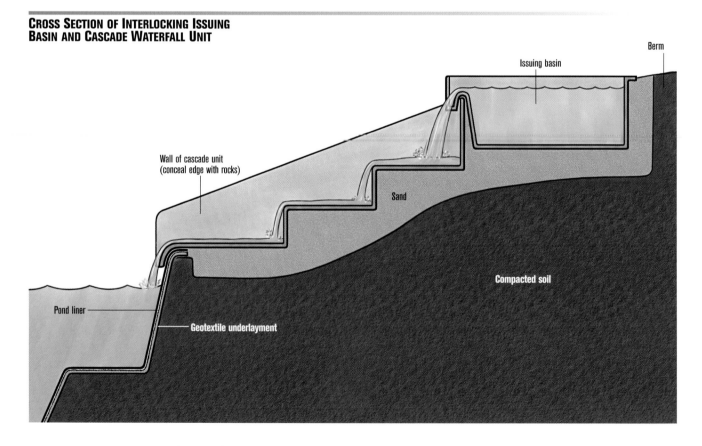

Berm

Issuing basin

Wall of cascade unit (conceal edge with rocks)

Sand

Compacted soil

Pond liner

Geotextile underlayment

Run tubing from the submerged pump to the connector piece of the waterfall. Use clamps at both ends to ensure a watertight connection. Adjust the position of the preformed waterfall to the exact spot you want. Then plug the pump into the power line to commence operation. Install flat spillway rock for the water's return to the pond. Backfill around the unit with soil or sand. Use decorative rocks and plants to blend the spillway into its surroundings.

Stair-step falls

A stair-step waterfall eliminates the header pools between cascades so the water moves quickly down the steps. A substantial volume of water is necessary for a continuous flow.

Calculate the rise and run for the steps and determine the materials you will need. A header pool or waterfall box is necessary at the top of the falls to feed the water to the steps in a wide, even swath. Water flowing directly from the pump hose, regardless of the volume, will not provide an even flow over the steps.

The steps may be constructed of stone, brick, pavers, concrete and decorative tile, or even timber treated with a nontoxic preservative. Use the same material for the spillways and edging.

The precision design for water flow along steps requires a strong and perfectly level foundation built with firmly compacted soil. Measure and stake out the design. Then cut the individual steps so they are smooth. Check that each step is level while sculpting the foundation. Firmly tamp any loose soil.

Cover the foundation of the steps with underlayment fabric. Then install flexible liner. Beginning with your catch basin or pond at the bottom, work your way up the falls one step at a time. Place the stone or other material you have selected on top of the liner.

Working from the bottom up, set each stone, brick, or timber in place and check them with a level. With all the pieces in place, test the flow with a garden hose and an additional gush of water poured from a bucket. When you are satisfied that your work is level and the flow will be adequate, use foam sealant or mortar to fuse the pieces to the liner and to each other. The sealant will keep the water in the channel and prevent it from flowing underneath or behind the stones or other

ELEVATION VIEW OF INTERLOCKING BASIN AND CASCADE WATERFALL

Berm · Carpenter's level · Berm · Cascade unit · Pond edge · Pond edge

construction materials. Black foam sealant is non-toxic once dry but mortar must be sealed with nontoxic sealant or latex paint once it dries.

Each spillway stone should project out to create a lip so that the water cascades over each step in a solid sheet. To prevent the water from flowing back along the underside of the spillway lip, attach a strip of fiberglass or metal to the edge of the spillway stone with waterproof construction adhesive. You can also cut a drip groove into the underside of the spillway stone.

INSTALLATION OF PREFORMED BASIN AND CASCADE

Rocks conceal edges and plumbing · Tubing for flexible pipe from pump to falls (covered with mulch or leftover soil)

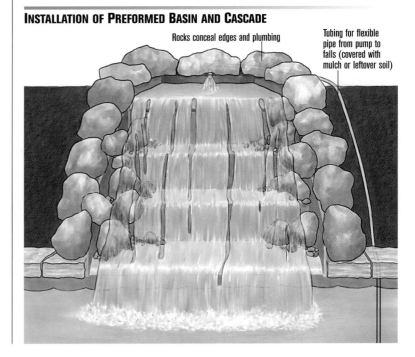

CONSTRUCTING A NATURALISTIC WATERFALL

Your primary concern in constructing a naturalistic rock- and plant-lined waterfall or stream will be to waterproof it. Most watercourses involve a flow of water between an upper basin, or header pool, and a lower, larger reservoir. It is possible to add a waterfall or watercourse to an existing pond.

Start by berming or terracing an inclined site for the size and shape of the planned waterfall. The site should be gently sloping and wide enough to accommodate the waterfall as well as the surrounding rocks and plants. Carefully level, line, and edge the watercourse to prevent water loss. Tamp the soil to prevent settling after the project is completed.

Multiple tiers

A header pool and spillway can be repeated along a slope, creating a series of descending falls and pools. Multiple-tier waterfalls offer dramatic cascading movement and sound.

To create multiple tiers, design the outline of the entire watercourse with a length of rope or a garden hose. Then mark the falls for each tier with stakes. Dig the base pond first and work your way up. Each spillway should create a 4- to 12-inch vertical drop between pools.

▲ Create multiple tiers for the most realistic effect.

◀ Fill the system and test the water flow before you trim the liner. You may need to adjust the sides near the falls.

The header pools must hold water when the pump is shut off for maintenance or in a power outage. The bottom of each header pool should slope away from the spillway, with a 12- to 15-inch depth in the back near the falls tapering up to a shallow 4- to 6-inch depth near the spillway. As you plan and dig the basins for the header pools, remember that the water volume of each pool will diminish when rocks are added. Varying the sizes of the header pools and the width of the weirs will create a more natural appearance. Consider splitting the flow on a tier, as described on page 99.

Taper the ledge of the spillway so it is deeper in the center to keep water from

MULTIPLE-CATARACT WATERFALL

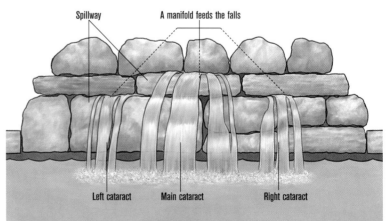

Spillway   A manifold feeds the falls

Left cataract   Main cataract   Right cataract

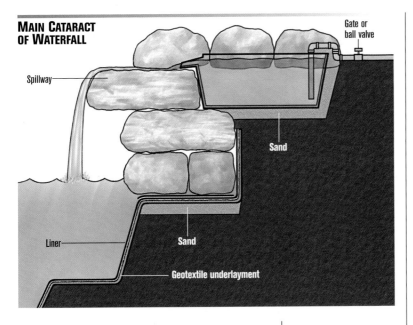

MAIN CATARACT OF WATERFALL

Gate or ball valve

Spillway

Sand

Liner

Sand

Geotextile underlayment

make any needed adjustments before you apply permanent sealant. Then choose a large, flat rock for the spillway. Place this rock so it projects 2 to 3 inches beyond the rockwork below it. Use sealant as necessary to prevent water from going under or around the spillway rock. Repeat these steps as you continue construction to the upper cascades.

After finishing the liner and rockwork, install the piping, beginning at the bottom reservoir and working up alongside the watercourse to the top falls. Allow at least two days for settling and curing before turning on the water to test the falls. Adjust the rockwork to alter the water flow rate, direction, and pattern. Place rocks in strategic spots to fine-tune the waterfall.

Arrange rocks and plants around the edge of the falls and pools to conceal the liner and direct the water flow. The rocks flanking the falls should be taller than the spillway to keep water in the channel.

spilling over the sides. Work bottom to top and overlap liners at the spillways.

After installing the liner and spillway stones for each cascade, fill the system with water. Take time to test the water flow before finishing the edges with rocks and trimming the liner. It may be necessary to build up the sides near the falls so the liner and stone shoulders will catch the splashing water.

Rockwork and plants

If your plans call for rocks over 200 pounds, plan ahead before installing the liner. Set concrete slabs or poured-concrete footings to support the weight of each heavy rock. Before the foundations set, cover them with geotextile material or carpet remnants.

Begin placing the rocks for the primary, or lowest, waterfall. Place all rocks and

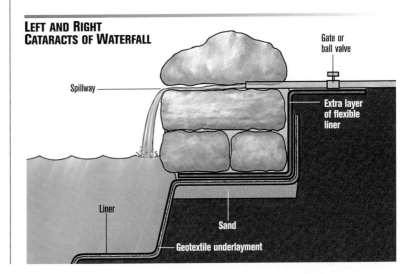

LEFT AND RIGHT CATARACTS OF WATERFALL

Gate or ball valve

Spillway

Extra layer of flexible liner

Liner

Sand

Geotextile underlayment

CHOOSING THE RIGHT PUMP

Calculate the total head to determine the size of pump needed for your waterfall. The head is the amount of resistance your pump works against.

Total head = static head + friction head

Static head (or rise) is the height, in feet, from the water's surface of the pond to the outlet at the top of the waterfall, stream, or spillway.

Friction head (or run) is the length of hose, in feet, from your pump to the outlet. A good general guideline is that 10 feet of hose equals 1 foot of friction head. With fittings, you can use a hose that is larger than the nozzle size coming off the pump. A larger hose will reduce friction head, but pumps work most efficiently with some

backpressure. The friction head can increase significantly if there are bends in the hose.

EXAMPLE:
Waterfall height 3' = static head 3'
Length of hose 20' = friction head 2'
Total head = 3' static head + 2' friction head = 5'

Check the pump performance rating on its package. While a pump may be rated for 1,800 gph, you need to know whether it can give you 1,500 gph with 5 feet of head.

If you need to convert feet of head to psi (pounds per square inch), divide by 2.3.

INSTALLING PLUMBING

KEEP CURRENT

Instructions given here apply to most filter units on the market when this book went to press. Consult the manufacturer's directions for the specific unit you purchase.

Placing the pump far from the waterfall promotes distribution of the freshly oxygenated water by maximizing circulation and filtration across the pond. Locating the pump under a waterfall, however, offers greater efficiency by allowing it to recirculate more water with less effort than if placed away from the waterfall.

Solid-handling pumps are designed to set directly on the bottom of the pond. Place other submersible pumps on bricks to keep them a few inches above potentially pump-clogging debris. If you want to control the water flow, install a ball valve on the pump outlet. Use a diverter (three-way) valve to control two features operated by the same pump.

Use a bulkhead connector through the liner wall to provide a flooded intake for a nonsubmersible pump. If the pump is not self-priming and is located above the pond's water level, install a foot valve (check valve) and a strainer on the intake pipe. Make a housing for the pump to lessen its noise.

Water lines

Use PVC flex pipe in areas where rocks or foot traffic might collapse thin vinyl tubing. It glues to regular schedule-40 PVC pipe and fittings. It has the strength of regular PVC pipe but its flexible nature allows you to avoid the use of elbows and other fittings to work around curved or irregular shapes.

Use flexible tubing or a hand-tight union connection to your pump. This allows easy access to the pump for servicing or removal. Clamp all other connections—especially any out-of-pond ones—to be watertight.

Position the line that feeds an issuing basin at the head of a waterfall or stream to release its flow under the water surface. Within the basin, consider using perforated tubing with an end cap. The line can enter the basin between the edging and the liner.

Mechanical filter hookup

Most mechanical filtration units work with water passing first through the filter and then through the pump. Make certain your pump and filter unit are compatible. Find the pump's intake by removing the intake screen. Screw a threaded male hose barb fitting into the pump's intake. Install a short length of flexible vinyl tubing between the pump and the filter. Secure both ends of the tubing with clamps. Some mechanical filters come with a built-in pump assembled, saving you the task.

Nonpressurized biofilters

Nearly all biological filters work outside of the pond without pressure. Because water discharged from one must flow by gravity, consider the site for it carefully. Locate a nonpressurized biofilter where

ANATOMY OF A STREAM WITH WATERFALLS

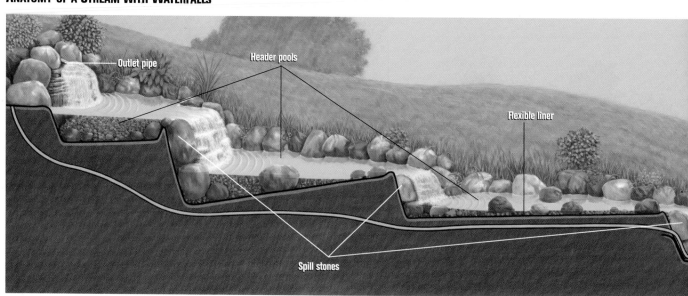

Outlet pipe
Header pools
Flexible liner
Spill stones

its discharge is higher than the level where the filtered water returns to the feature. Possible return points include under the edging of a pond, stream, or bog garden or at the top of a waterfall. Allow easy access to it for servicing.

Make sure the biofilter sits securely on a level base. Connect PVC flex pipe or rigid PVC pipe (as appropriate) for inflow and discharge lines. These conduct water from the pump into the biofilter and from the biofilter to the discharge point. Operate the pump to verify that the connections are watertight.

Pressurized biofilter hookup

A pressurized biofilter can be located almost anywhere and is easily concealed in a garage, under the deck, or in a buried vault. Smaller models operate with submersible pumps. These small pressurized units are often buried adjacent to the pond with only their top cap exposed for servicing. Larger pressurized filters utilize more powerful nonsubmersible pumps.

Connect the pond's bottom drain to the filter intake. Then connect the filter outlet to a nonsubmersible, flooded-suction pump or self-priming pump. Pipe the pump's discharge to the filter's back-flush valve. Connect the discharge on the back-flush valve to a water line for release of the filtered water back to a waterfall, stream, or pond. Pipe the waste connection on the back-flush valve to a drain or any suitable discharge area for release of the nutrient-rich back-flush water. Start the pump and check the operation of the filter.

In-ground filter hookup

Make careful measurements to ensure that the unit top is slightly above the pond's water level when you set it in the excavation.

Install a level tamped-sand base, concrete slab, or poured concrete footing on which the filter can rest. Make the installation in tandem with the pond construction. Water will exit the pond through one or more bottom drains. A nonsubmersible pump at the end of the filter train sucks water through the system. The water level in the filter will match the pond's water level.

Filtered water travels from the filter through piping to the nonsubmersible pump. The pump draws water from the filter and forces it through piping to a waterfall, stream, bog garden, or pond. Install drain lines equipped with knife valves at the bottom of each filter chamber. Combine multiple drain lines into a single line to direct filtered water to a lower point or a sump pump. Create access from the ground's surface to the buried knife valve handles with vertically aligned piping.

Recheck the level of the components and backfill around the filter. Turn the water on. Fill the filter with water, and then start the pump for a trial run.

Pump
Weatherproof electrical outlet
Flexible tubing
Pond

AERATION WITHOUT A FOUNTAIN

If you want a bubbly fountain effect without buying and installing a fountain, place the discharge pipe of your submersible pump an inch or so below the water's surface. Adjust the discharge closer to the surface for a livelier effect. Lower it for more subdued results.

INSTALLING LIGHTS

HINT

When planning your water features, consider installing a remote switch inside the house. You'll be able to turn on the falls, fountains, and lights without going outside.

Whenever possible, position out-of-water lights to conceal their housings and cords: underneath a deck, behind a rock, or tucked into the foliage of a shrub.

Whatever type of lighting you choose, be sensitive to its effect on the neighbors. Don't let the lights shine in their windows.

Low-voltage outdoor lighting

Low-voltage lights offer many advantages. They are easy to install and change, use less energy than 120-volt lighting, don't require complicated precautions or configurations, give you more flexibility in your lighting options, and are intrinsically safe. Their initial cost is modest compared to the alternatives. Installation of a low-voltage lighting system does not require the services of a licensed electrician. It's a simple do-it-yourself project. Often used with residential water features, low-voltage lights require an electrical transformer that converts regular household 120-volt current into safer 12-volt power. The lights and transformer are sold together in kits along with additional modular pieces. Here's what you'll need: a transformer, a power cable, stakes for placement in the ground or holders for placement in water, a set of lights, a set of 12-volt bulbs, and optional colored lenses. Some kits include a timer that turns the lights on and off. Check the wattage of the transformer to determine the maximum number of lights it can support. You may want to add more lights later without having to buy another transformer.

Consider your options, and then decide the location of each light. Measure carefully so that you can determine which components or kit you need. Follow the instructions that come with the kit or lighting pieces. Setup usually involves attaching a low-voltage cable to the transformer, laying the cable, and attaching lights where desired along the cable. Plug the transformer into a GFCI outlet when you want to turn on the lights. For wiring simplicity, install a transformer with a built-in timer.

One rule in placing lights is never to let them shine directly on the water because they will create a harsh glare. In-pond lights need fairly clear water to be effective. Murky water blocks too much light and considerably diminishes the light's effectiveness. If you have fish in your water garden, leave dark areas where they can retreat from the light. Fish need these crevices for refuge. For best effect, and to be kind to the fish, never light the entire pond for nighttime viewing.

▲ **When installing lighting in your water garden, leave the cords long enough to pull the lights out of the pond for easy maintenance access. Coil the excess cords and hide them under the rocks.**

INSTALLING LOW-VOLTAGE LIGHTING

Installation of low-voltage landscape lights is a snap, even for beginners. They're safer than 120-volt lights because of their low voltage. Many low-voltage lighting systems are sold as kits, complete with instructions.

Hooking up a low-voltage system starts with installing a transformer, which reduces household current from 120 volts to 12 volts. Install the transformer near the GFCI receptacle closest to the water feature, following the manufacturer's instructions. Even 12-volt systems should use a GFCI unit to prevent shocks. Most transformers are mounted next to an outlet and plugged into it.

Run exterior electrical cable from the transformer to the lights. It's important to choose a cable with the right size wire for the total wattage of the bulbs in the system. Add the total watts of each bulb supplied by the cable: 14-gauge wire can handle up to 144 watts, 12-gauge up to 192 watts, and 10-gauge up to 288 watts.

Bury the cable several inches underground, running it through a length of PVC pipe for extra protection from tillers and spades.

Then attach the lights to the cable. Some lights attach with clips while others must be wired into the system. Refer to the instructions that come with the lights.

Line-voltage lighting

Large deep pools generally require the more intense light that comes from line-voltage (120-volt) lighting. Although it has the power to provide brilliant lighting, line-voltage lighting can be used for the same purposes as low-voltage lighting. Enlist an electrical contractor or swimming pool contractor to install submersible lights into the walls of a concrete pool.

Solar lighting

To avoid installation of electrical wires for lighting, consider using solar lights that convert sunlight into electricity and store it in batteries. Solar lights turn on automatically at night or on dark days. Models are available for use in or out of water. Floating solar lights also can be used as pond ornaments.

Solar bulbs are bright and do not burn out like other bulbs. Their operating times depend on your geographic location and daily weather. During extended cloudy conditions, they may not function well.

TIPS FOR SUCCESSFUL LIGHTING

1. Install underwater lights directly below a waterfall or fountain. Aim light in the same direction as the water's motion to highlight it.
2. Install ground lighting so that it shines away from the observer. Pathway lights should focus on the ground or nearby plants or ornaments and present no visual glare.
3. Low-voltage underwater bulbs are typically 20 watts. Low-voltage garden lightbulbs are usually 10 or 12 watts. Underwater and garden bulbs may be used interchangeably. However, if you are using a low-voltage garden light set that powers six ground lights and decide to add one underwater light, you will have to cut back to only four of the ground lights to avoid overloading the circuit.
4. Avoid directing lights to shine on the water's surface, creating glare. Use the water as a reflecting pool by leaving the surface dark and lighting the surrounding landscaping instead.
5. Periodic cleaning of submersible light lenses keeps them performing at their best.
6. Install lighting around your water feature before you finish landscaping, such as laying sod or adding mulch or gravel.
7. Spotlight an unusual specimen such as a night-blooming tropical water lily to show off its special attraction. Avoid spotlighting a night bloomer from below. More subtle side lighting works better.
8. If a low-voltage light fails to work when you test the set, check that there is contact with the power cable.
9. Mount the transformer to a vertical stake set in concrete for stability.
10. Low-voltage lighting works best in small gardens because each lamp lights a small area. Standard-voltage systems are more valuable in areas where brilliant illumination provides safety or security.

▲ Aim in-water lights away from the viewer and in the same direction as the water's motion.

INSTALLING EDGING

Whether you choose some form of rock, wood, or plants for edging depends on the style and function of your water feature. Rock and stone are the most common and natural edging materials. Review the edging options described on pages 56 and 57. Consider the functional aspects of standing or sitting on edging to view, maintain, or otherwise access the water feature.

Rock and stone

When edging a pond with a preformed liner or using heavy stonework on a flexible liner, build a masonry collar under the edge for adequate support. On a 2-inch layer of gravel, set a collar of concrete block or flat

▲ **Construct drystack masonry with pockets to hold small plants to create lively edging that changes with the seasons.**

rock in a 1-inch layer of mortar. Extend the liner over the collar. Then spread underlayment on top of it before setting the rock edging in place. Scatter smaller stones between and behind the rocks to create a natural look. Randomly set larger, partially buried rocks behind the edging to complete the effect.

Place heavy edging rocks (weighing more than 150 pounds) on the ground around the perimeter of the water feature. Mortar or concrete isn't necessary as long as the rocks are situated in stable positions. Create a firm foundation for lighter-weight stonework edging by spreading a 3-inch layer of crushed rock. Top that with a 1-inch layer of concrete or mortar before setting the stones in place.

Concrete, mortar, and pH

Mortar or concrete used for stabilizing edging is alkaline. Pond water and rain that splash these materials will wash lime into the water, which causes an increase in pH levels dangerous or even fatal to fish. You can neutralize the concrete or mortar by scrubbing it with a stiff brush and diluted vinegar. Scrub and rinse the neutralized areas several times, using water from a garden hose. Then pump the rinse water out of the pond. A single treatment should fix the problem.

EDGING TIP

Here's a good way to prevent the liner from showing. Dig the edging shelf deep enough for a double layer of flagstones, cut stones, bricks, or other edging. Lay the first layer of edging, then wrap the liner over the first layer as shown and top with the second. Water can now be filled to the middle of the first layer of edging. With one layer of edging, the water can be filled only a little below the bottom of the edging.

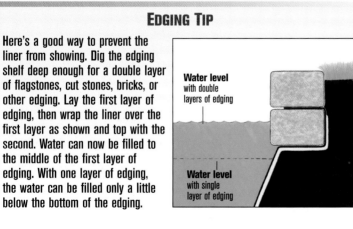

Water level with double layers of edging

Water level with single layer of edging

Brick

Before laying a brick edge, make sure the perimeter of the water feature is level. A single layer of brick requires a 3-inch-thick foundation of crushed rock. Use paver bricks—the solid ones, not the ones with holes—as edging to minimize the invasion of weeds and grass among the edgers. Apply mortar under and between the bricks to make a sturdy edge.

Wood

Set wood posts or logs vertically in concrete to form a pier edging. Use water-resistant wood planks or recycled-plastic "lumber" to build a deck or walkway along the water feature or jutting into it. Set the construction on concrete footings.

CONCEALED EDGE CONSTRUCTION

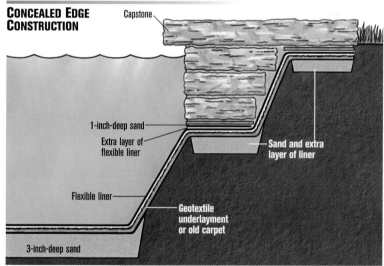

Capstone

1-inch-deep sand

Extra layer of flexible liner

Sand and extra layer of liner

Flexible liner

Geotextile underlayment or old carpet

3-inch-deep sand

▲ Secure the lip around a formal pool with mortar under and between the bricks or stones.

beds of wildflowers are also excellent edgers. Choose plants suited to your climate as well as to your garden's conditions, including sunlight, soil, and moisture level. Stagger three, five, or seven plants around in clusters for effective results. Place tall plants on the far side of the water feature where they won't obstruct your view. Keep plantings simple: Too many different plants can create a busy, confusing scene.

Turf and plants

Turf makes a neat edging but can get messy if soil washes out of the lawn into the water feature or if grass clippings blow into the water when you mow. Prepare the edge for a lawn by excavating a shallow trench around the perimeter of the water feature and letting the liner extend into it. Cover the flap of liner in the trench with soil. Lay sod over the trench to finish the edge.

Intersperse plantings with rocks and stones to create a naturalistic edge. Avoid ringing the water feature with a single strand of rocks like a necklace. Choose easy-care plants, such as low-growing evergreens, irises, and hostas. Groundcovers and small

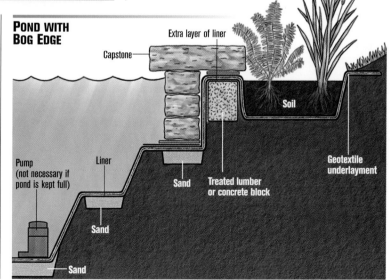

POND WITH BOG EDGE

Extra layer of liner

Capstone

Soil

Pump (not necessary if pond is kept full)

Liner

Sand

Treated lumber or concrete block

Geotextile underlayment

Sand

Sand

MAINTENANCE

A well-designed water garden should take minimal time to maintain. Unless you have a very large water feature or a fish-only pond, you'll spend about an hour or less each week monitoring water quality, feeding fish, and grooming plants. When estimating the amount of time to budget for maintenance, plan on about 10 minutes per thousand gallons of water per week.

Completely emptying and cleaning the water feature on a regular basis isn't necessary, nor is it advisable. In fact, frequent emptying and cleaning can cause more harm than good. It can injure your fish as they try to adjust to varying water temperatures and conditions. It can destroy and wash away beneficial bacteria, which can take days, even weeks, to reestablish. Unless the pond is very dirty from too many fish or too many decaying leaves in the water, most ponds need to be completely drained, cleaned, and refilled only once every few years.

Fishponds require more care to keep fish wastes from fouling the water and to maintain fish health. Plan on spending extra time cleaning filters (which remove the wastes), skimming debris from the surface, and making sure the pumps that aerate and recirculate water are working.

If your water garden takes too much time to maintain, it may have a fundamental problem in its design or construction or in the ratio of plants, fish, and water. You will save time and money if you identify and correct the basic problem instead of spending hours each week fixing its side effects. If you can't determine the source of the problem, consult a professional water garden specialist.

As long as the pond has no major problems, you will do most of your work in spring and fall. Chores include dividing plants, returning them to the pond, and removing dead foliage. In fall you need to ready the pond for winter. These few extra hours in spring and fall give you time to enjoy your water garden in the summer with only a little grooming required. Your water will stay clear, your fish healthy, and your plants lush.

◀ **Most ponds rarely need to be drained entirely for cleaning or repairs. As long as the ecosystem is in balance, just a few maintenance tasks in fall and spring will prepare your water garden for a summer of enjoyment.**

FUNDAMENTALS

Ponds in the wild contain a complex network of checks and balances that generally maintain pond health without help. Garden ponds have the same network but, being artificial, require your assistance.

If your pond is out of balance, it will give you signals: bad odors, fish dying or gasping for breath at the surface, dark or green water, and stunted and diseased plants. Here's how to help keep your garden pond healthy.

■ **Use all the elements:** Plants and other pond life work together. Fish are not required in the water garden but do consume mosquito larvae. They add lively interest to the pond. Floating plants provide shade. They cool and filter the water and control algae. Submerged plants are also filters and feed fish as well as create shelter and spawning areas for them. Use one bunch of submerged plants for every 2 square feet of pond surface.

■ **Know your water:** Invest in a kit for testing pond water. Various inexpensive kits are readily available. Test for ammonia and nitrite levels when you first fill your pond. Then check periodically, particularly if fish look stressed or are dying. If the

▲ **Spreading bird netting over the pond in autumn is a simple way to catch leaves and make cleanup easier. Hold the netting in place with bricks or stones. You can also use one of the cloth leaf covers available as a pond cover.**

◄ **Periodically use an inexpensive pond water test kit to measure water quality. Add water if hot weather causes excessive evaporation. Aerate the water with a fountain or falls to help maintain water clarity.**

pond develops a chemical imbalance, a partial water change, described below, will lower ammonia and nitrite levels.

■ **Keep the pond filled:** A drop of an inch or more below the normal water level can lead to unhealthy concentrations of salts and minerals and can expose the liner to deteriorating UV rays. Evaporation may require you to add water to the pond.

When you add water, fill the pond with just a trickle from the hose (keep it at the bottom of the pond) to allow fish and other pond life to adapt to the gradual changes in temperature and pH. Add no more than 10 to 20 percent of the total volume at any one time or the fish could go into shock. If using municipal water, add chlorine remover to the pond whenever you top it off.

Partially change the water when needed. Although it's best to keep the pond filled, salt and waste materials build up in the water over time, despite refills. To freshen the pond, drain it by about 10 percent of its capacity, preferably by drawing water from the bottom, where concentrations of harmful substances are highest. Then refill it as described. Do this right before a rain, if possible, so rainfall can replace at least some of the water.

■ **Provide aeration:** Whether from a fountain or a waterfall, splashing water keeps the pond well oxygenated, which is essential for maintaining healthy fish. Oxygenated water also stays fresh, warding off foul-smelling bacteria that thrive in a low-oxygen environment.

Clarifiers

Flocculating clarifiers are designed to eliminate cloudy water created by algae and dirt. These products cause detritus suspended in the water, including algae, to clump together and fall to the bottom of the water feature, where they decay. Lighter-weight particles float. Mechanical filtration, vacuuming, and skimming easily remove the heavier particles. Results of this treatment show quickly, often within 24 hours. Dense algae growth requires an additional treatment or two, spaced one week apart. Potent for only a day, the liquid clarifier destroys only algae growing on the day of application. Apply it again when algae reappear.

Barley straw

Barley straw placed in a pond or stream prevents algae growth when introduced in the spring before algae appear. As the straw decomposes, it releases substances that convert to hydrogen peroxide when exposed to oxygen and sunlight. Peroxide inhibits algae growth but evaporates quickly. Barley straw in the water produces a continuous supply of peroxide for up to six months. It is safe for plants and fish.

Use about three-tenths of an ounce of barley straw or pellets for each square yard of water surface. Bundle it loosely in net bags or nylon stockings, and attach corks or plastic floats to keep the bundles from sinking. Barley straw works its magic near the surface where there is more oxygen.

▲ **Fish food and other wastes result in nitrates, which algae thrive upon. Tame out-of-control algae with filters or a UV clarifier.**

■ **Remove leaves and debris:** Debris decomposes and fouls water if not removed. Skim leaves, fallen petals, and other floating plant matter from the bottom and surface of the pond with a net or by hand.

Pinch off yellowing and dying leaves. Make skimming the pond a daily routine. In autumn, put netting over the pond to catch falling leaves. In late fall, when you remove the pump for the winter, clear the water of debris before the pond ices over.

■ **Keep it under control:** If fish numbers get out of hand, give some away. Regularly thin aggressive plants. Divide overgrown plants so no one element takes over.

■ **Consider a filter:** If the garden pond has continuing problems with debris, too much light, or excessive fish waste, consider adding a biological filter to the pond setup.

■ **Prevent runoff:** When fertilizing or applying other chemicals to the lawn and plants surrounding your garden pond, don't let the materials run off or trickle into the water. They can be toxic to fish and may promote algae growth in the water.

■ **Feed fish properly:** Feeding too much or too often fouls the water and necessitates a larger filter. Feed fish only when they are ravenous and give them only as much as they can eat in a few minutes.

▲ **String algae remove fish waste but may quickly take over if too many nutrients are present in the water. Remove excess string algae with an algae brush or toilet bowl brush tied to a pole.**

WATER TREATMENTS

Think of water treatments as you would prescription drugs. Avoid them if possible but use them as directed when necessary. Use only treatments designed for water gardens if you raise aquatic plants, ornamental fish, scavengers, and unseen-yet-beneficial nitrifying bacteria. Algae-control treatments and water-test kits for swimming pools work well in swimming pools, but these treatments kill all water garden life. The pool test kits will not indicate what a pond-keeper needs to know.

▼ Keep a pond-water treatment kit on hand if you use public water and keep fish. Chemicals used to treat the water will kill the fish. Treat the water each time you top off the pond.

Chlorine and chloramine removal

Check with your local utility to learn what chemicals are used to treat public water. Chloramine (chlorine combined with ammonia) is most commonly used and will kill fish. Chloramine, a powerful antibacterial agent, remains in water for months, making treatment mandatory if fish are to survive. Chloramine shows up on the ammonia test in a pond-water test kit. Weekly monitoring for ammonia could keep your fish healthy. Add chloramine treatment (which also removes chlorine) each time you top off the pond. If you add about 5 percent of the water volume, treat the pond with 5 percent of the quantity needed to treat the entire pond. Fortunately, chlorine and chloramine removal treatments work almost instantly. Follow label instructions.

Chlorine naturally escapes when exposed to the atmosphere, making pond water fish-safe two to three days after the water is drawn. If you're adding less than 10 percent to the volume of water already in the pond, there is no need to dechlorinate. However, if you're increasing the volume of water by more than 10 percent, add dechlorination treatment to neutralize chlorine.

Fish-keepers who use public water need to maintain sufficient antichlorine or antichloramine treatment for a complete water change. Discovery of toxic matter in the water, a massive leak, or an accidental overflow of water call for the immediate use of these water-quality treatments.

Beneficial bacteria

Beneficial nitrifying bacteria remove ammonia and nitrite from the water. They colonize around whatever surface areas they find in the pond. To enhance their effectiveness and speed their development, add concentrated bacteria to the biological filter and around the pond itself. These bacteria are sold in dry and liquid forms. The more expensive liquid form acts more quickly but has a shorter shelf life. Once in the pond or biofilter, the bacteria produce no noticeable smell.

Using a test kit is usually simple: you add a reactive chemical agent to a pond-water sample or dip treated paper strips into the water and compare the results with a chart.

Most test kits don't measure the level of dissolved oxygen in the water. If oxygen is low, however, the fish tell you by gasping at the surface. Other water-quality deficiencies may also cause them to gasp. Once you become comfortable with the daily readings from a water-quality test kit, weekly checks will suffice. As you learn to recognize the behavior patterns of your fish, you'll be able to read their signs too.

Water-quality test kits: a life-and-death matter

Fish may die when water quality becomes compromised. Test kits enable you to check pond water for unsafe levels of certain chemicals. For example, when ammonia and nitrate reach toxic levels, fish become listless, uninterested in eating, and vulnerable to disease and parasite attack. Chlorine and chloramine must be removed. Ammonia and nitrite levels must be low. Stress becomes a threat if pH is under 6.5 or over 8.5. As pH increases, ammonia becomes much more potent and more likely to kill fish. Check the fishpond levels daily in midmorning.

▲ When refilling your pond with tap water add chloramine remover before restocking it with fish.

▲ Bundle loose barley straw or pellets in net bags and float them on the pond. The decomposing barley produces peroxide, which inhibits algae growth. The barley may last up to six months in the pond.

WHEN APPLYING ALGAE CONTROL

When you use an algae-control agent, your pond water loses oxygen as it is absorbed by the killed, decaying algae. The decaying algae may consume so much oxygen that the fish become stressed or possibly suffocate. Monitor fish for signs of stress, such as gasping at the surface or listlessness. Aerating the water with a waterfall, a fountain, air stones, or water sprayed through the air from a garden hose into the pond makes up for the oxygen depletion. Be especially alert to this potential situation when the water temperature is over 80°F. As the temperature rises, fish consume more oxygen but the water holds less.

KEEPING THE POND CLEAN

▶ Use a soft brush to clean the surface of the liner gently. Hose down the liner and remove the dirty water before refilling the pond.

L ate summer to early fall is the best time to clean ponds. Clean fishponds on a cool day, which is easier on fish, at least a month before winter sets in to give the fish enough time to recover. In warm climates, wait until plants go dormant and the water temperature is 60°F.

First, place a holding tank for fish in the shade and fill it with pond water. Use a 30-gallon trash can, stock tank, or a child's wading pool. Begin to drain the pond. You can bail the water, or replace the output piping on the pond's submersible pump with a hose. Run the hose out of the pond and siphon the water. While you wait for the level to drop, clean the filters.

A nearly empty pond makes it easier to catch fish. Net them when the water is drained to 6 inches and place them in a bucket of pond water. After catching a few, transfer them to the holding pen. Cover the holding pen with netting so the fish won't jump out. Don't feed the fish at this time. If they are going to be held for more than an hour in the holding pen, put an aerator in the container.

Continue to remove water until only several inches remain in the bottom of the pond. Then stop pumping and check the muck for small fish, frogs, tadpoles, and other animals. Put these in the bucket also.

Next, remove the plants. Their foliage must be kept wet or at least damp so they can survive. You can wrap foliage and pots in wet newspaper and set plants in the shade, or submerge them in the wading pool or in buckets of water.

Bail the remaining water and pour it onto flower beds and the rest of the landscape. Don't pour it down a drain because it will clog the plumbing. Scoop mud from the pond bottom, taking care not to damage the liner. Dump the mud on the compost pile. A wet-dry shop vacuum with the filter removed works well to remove muck, water, and other debris.

Once the pond is empty, hose it down. Use a soft brush to clean the sides of the liner. Scrubbing also removes beneficial bacteria and helpful algae, so don't scrub too thoroughly. After hosing down the pond, remove the dirty water. Make any necessary repairs, especially if you have detected a leak.

Next, fill the pond about halfway and add the plants. Then continue filling the pond, preparing the water in the same way as for the pool's first stocking, with chlorine and chloramine removers, if necessary. Return frogs and scavengers to the pond. Check the fish for disease, and treat them accordingly. Then gently place them in plastic bags with water from the holding tank. Inflate and seal the bags. Float the bags on the surface until the water temperature inside the bag is close to the pond temperature. Another method is to gradually add fresh pond water to the temporary holding pen. Either way, when the container's water temperature is within 2°F of the pond's, you can release the fish safely. Returning some of the water from the bucket and holding pen to the pond will add beneficial microorganisms.

SEASONAL MAINTENANCE

Spring checklist

The pond

▪ Vacuum or sweep the pond bottom if there is a significant accumulation of leaves and other detritus. Otherwise, drain the pond while removing its denizens, remove the accumulation, and rinse—don't wash—the pond before carefully restocking it, following the directions on page 86.

▪ If a cloud of algae blooms, don't panic. This seasonal adjustment of the ecosystem is a natural occurrence.

▪ Collect and add rainwater to top off the pond. Rainwater contains fewer chemicals than tap water.

Equipment

▪ Reconnect the pump and filter, if stored over winter.

▪ Check lights and electrical connections. Make any necessary repairs.

▪ Inspect the liner for tears or punctures. Make any necessary repairs.

▪ Start a biological filter by adding beneficial nitrifying bacteria when the pond water temperature reaches 53°F–57°F.

▪ Replace the bulb in the UV clarifier and reinstall it.

Plants

▪ Clean up, weed, and mulch peripheral landscape beds.

▪ Return hardy aquatic plants to the pond if you removed them for the winter. If you overwintered them in the deepest part of the pond, relocate them to their plant shelves for the growing season.

▪ Add new marginal, submerged, and floating plants.

▪ Divide root-bound plants and repot the divisions. Share extras with your water gardening friends.

Fish

▪ As water begins to warm and fish resume activity, feed them minimally with a spring/fall high-carbohydrate food.

▪ Inspect fish closely, looking especially for signs of parasites, sores, or lethargic behavior. If you have never added salt to your pond, add 1 pound of salt (solar, sea, or kosher; no iodine) per 100 gallons of water over a two- to four-day period. If you see symptoms of a fish disease or parasite, eliminate it with an aquatic remedy.

▪ Test for ammonia and nitrite weekly. If levels are high, decrease feeding fish food until the biofilter takes effect and the ammonia and nitrite levels drop. If levels continue rising, use an ammonia-absorbing zeolite package in the waterfall-issuing basin or filter.

▪ Add nitrifying bacteria to guard against potentially toxic buildup of ammonia from fish waste.

◀ In spring, top off the pond with collected rainwater, which contains fewer chemicals than tap water.

◀ Remove weeds regularly in summer and clean the pump intake each week to make sure it is free of plant debris. Spray water from a garden hose to wash down algae accumulated on the pond liner.

Summer checklist

The pond

■ Any change in the rate of water flowing from a feature or filter indicates a clog in a pump intake or filter, kinked tubing, or a blocked water line. Keep water recirculating continuously through a biological filter. Recirculating water and increased oxygen in the water are vital to the health of your fish in hot weather.

■ If your pond consistently loses more than an inch of water per week, check for a leak. Begin by examining the waterfall or any other feature outside the pond walls, where most leaks appear. Leave the waterfalls off. If the pond level remains constant, the leak is almost certainly in the waterfall or pipelines to it. Otherwise, check the pond walls and bottom for leaks. If there are none, add water sprayed through the air from a garden hose to replace what has evaporated.

■ Control algae naturally using submerged and floating plants. A properly sized ultraviolet clarifier turns green water clear within a day. Use a rake or algae brush to remove filamentous algae.

▼ **Install netting to catch fallen leaves or remove them each day with a skimmer. Remove any sediment from the pond bottom before the weather turns cold.**

Equipment

■ Clean the pump intake weekly or as needed. Clean the filter, skimmer, and light lenses as needed for efficient operation.

Plants

■ Regularly remove excessive plant growth, yellowing or damaged leaves, and spent flowers.

■ Rake off floating plants if they cover more than 60 percent of the water's surface or cover the crowns of marginal plants.

■ Pick off pests or blast them off plants using cold water from the garden hose. Remove and dispose of diseased plants.

Fish

■ As the water temperature rises above 60°F, switch from high-carbohydrate fish food to a high-protein product.

■ Test the water weekly, checking the levels of pH, ammonia, and nitrite. If the pH rises above 8 or falls below 6.8 and remains there, add a pond remedy designed to adjust pH in the needed direction by 0.1 point per day to reach the normal range.

■ Fish gasping at the surface of the water may indicate poor water quality. However, it can indicate other problems, such as improper pH. Do what you can to increase oxygen. Keep the waterfall or fountain running continuously. Alleviate a moderate level of toxicity by removing one-third of the water. Replace it with water sprayed through the air from a garden hose (to release chlorine and absorb oxygen). If you use public water, add antichlorine or antichloramine treatment to the pond and replace no more than one-third of the pond's volume at a time.

■ Netting, electric fencing, scarecrows, imitation snakes and owls, and motion detectors connected to impulse sprinklers may deter predators. A watchful dog works most effectively.

Autumn checklist

Equipment

■ Install netting over the pond to prevent falling leaves from landing in the water and decaying.

■ If you don't install netting, use a skimmer to remove leaves daily. Use a vacuum or leaf sweeper to remove leaves from the pond bottom. If an inch or more of sediment has accumulated on the bottom, clean the pond before the weather turns cold.

CLEANING HINT

Fall is the best time to clean the pond. Removing fallen leaves before they foul the water benefits fish all winter. Mild autumn temperatures and end-of-season robust health make it easier for the fish to withstand the stress associated with being handled.

■ If you live in an area where the pond can freeze solid, remove, clean, and store your mechanical and biofilters and pumps, when the water temperature drops below 45°F. Store submersible pumps in a bucket of water to prevent the seals from drying out. Install a thermostatically controlled floating pond heater anywhere in the pond. Change the water source from bottom drain to skimmer.

■ Drain pipes to prevent them from freezing and cracking. Turn off the water supply until spring.

Plants

■ Remove floating and tropical plants when frost makes them unsightly. Save tropical lilies in a greenhouse pool. Transfer hardy water lilies to deeper water where they won't freeze or store them wrapped in moist newspaper in plastic bags in a cool, dark area, such as a root cellar or an old working refrigerator.

■ Remove and overwinter tropical marginal plants indoors.

■ Cut upright marginal plant stalks 1 to 2 inches above the water surface (wait until spring to cut cattails and grasses). Remove excessive growth of submerged plants.

Fish

■ When the water temperature drops below 60°F in cold climates, switch from summer's high-protein fish food to the high-carbohydrate spring and autumn food. Reduce feeding to every third day. Stop feeding fish at 50°F or lower.

Winter checklist

Equipment

■ Remove the leaf netting to avoid snow buildup.

■ Prevent the pond from freezing solid if it contains fish and plants. Remove the inhabitants and partially drain the feature or install a pond deicer.

■ Smashing the ice or melting it with boiling water can harm the fish.

■ Operating the pump during freezing weather can damage the pump, the pipes, and the fish. Allow the pump to continue working only if you live in a mild climate where ice is a temporary occurrence.

■ In cold climates, shut down waterfalls. Disconnect and store the pump until spring. A power outage in winter can ruin equipment left running.

■ Protect a raised pond from ice damage by draining it to ground level or use a deicer.

Plants

■ Leave the dead foliage of grasses and other perennials to stand at the edge of the water feature. This aids plant survival and offers protection for birds in winter.

■ After the ground freezes, mulch around plants at the edge the water to preserve soil moisture and protect plants from the damage of winter's freeze–thaw cycle.

Fish

■ Discontinue feeding fish when the water temperature drops below 50°F. Resist the temptation to feed them during any midwinter warm periods.

▲ If snow and ice are common in your climate, shut down your pump for the winter to avoid damaging it and hurting the fish.

REPAIRING A LEAK

▲ Repair kits are available to patch leaks in flexible or rigid pond liners.

Before draining the water to locate a leak, make sure the loss is not due to normal evaporation or a leaking waterfall. If the pond is near a building that reflects heat, is located in full sun, or has a large fountain or falls, evaporation may be the cause. Water levels also drop more quickly on hot or windy days. Aquatic plants increase evaporation too. Put a bucket filled with water near your water garden and watch the level for a day or two to make an informal measurement of evaporation.

Leak detection

If the water level in your feature drops more than 1 to 1½ inches per week, you have a leak. Waterfalls and streams are the source of most leaks. Shut off the waterfall or stream so that you can isolate a leak. Top off the pond. Wait 24 hours, then check the water level. If the pond is full, then the leak is in the waterfall or stream.

If the pond loses water while the waterfall and stream are turned off, look for the leak by adding a trace of food coloring to the water. Sometimes dye makes a slow steady leak visible. Another method involves allowing the water level to drop until it stops. At that point, examine the liner's perimeter and mark the water level using a crayon or chalk.

Pump out another few inches of water if the reduced water pressure results in a slower leak. This also permits closer scrutiny of the suspected area. Monitor the dropping water level and relocate pond inhabitants to temporary quarters. The water level will sink to the bottom if that's where the leak exists. You might find the leak on the bottom even if the water drop stops a few inches above it. Wherever the leak is, clean the area before examining it.

Flexible liner leaks

Before making repairs, determine what caused a puncture. Remove any sharp objects under the liner and add fresh sand there if necessary. Clean the area around the leak with a solvent such as paint thinner and a plastic abrasive pad or steel wool (to promote a better bond between patching materials), and allow it to dry. Use a scrap of liner to make a patch.

Apply a thin coat of PVC glue (made for flexible PVC) to the patch for a PVC pond liner. Center the patch over the tear and apply uniform pressure on the patch with a wallpaper roller or a rolling pin. After 12 hours, refill the pond. For a punctured EPDM or butyl flexible liner, use a liner repair kit with adhesive-faced patches. If possible, insert a board behind the area being repaired. Remove the protective paper from the adhesive face and apply the patch over the hole. Apply uniform pressure over the face of the patch with a wallpaper roller or rolling pin.

If a tear has caused a leak, apply two-sided liner sealing tape in a rectangular shape around the tear. Apply a patch of liner material of the same rectangular size. Roll over the patch to secure it (as described above). Apply single-sided liner seaming tape over the edges of the patch.

Waterfall and stream leaks

Settling under a waterfall or stream liner causes water loss outside the area covered by the liner. In this case, disassemble the feature and rebuild it accordingly. Rodents may have chewed a hole in the liner. Maturing plants can cause water to rise higher than what the liner can control. Look for moist soil along the outside edge of the liner and repair as needed.

Repair a crack or puncture in a fiberglass unit using a fiberglass repair kit. Find the damaged area and repair it to prevent a recurring leak. Roughen the area around the leak with sandpaper. Apply a resin-soaked mesh patch according to the repair-kit instructions. If your water garden supplier doesn't stock the repair kit, check with a boat or auto supply store.

Maintenance Equipment

Autumn leaves drifting on the water surface may look attractive but can foul the water and threaten the health of your fish. A leaf skimmer is a flat, netlike device that you sweep across the water to collect fallen, floating leaves. Ideally, its handle reaches halfway across your pond. Some skimmers come with a handle. Others require that you add one. The same handle (either fixed length or telescopic) that you buy separately for the skimmer can be used with a pond vacuum and a fishnet.

Fishnets

Fishnets typically are made of long-lasting nylon or cotton with ⅛- to 1/16-inch openings. These nets are softer and thus gentler for fish. The fishnet should be at least as wide as the longest fish in your pond. A deep net gives you better control than a shallow one when catching fish.

Healthy fish easily evade most overt attempts to net them out of a pond. Experienced fish-keepers slowly maneuver the net under the fish as the fish eagerly eat floating fish food, catching them unaware. Koi-keepers use a net to guide a fish into a plastic pan, then carry the fish in the pan to its next location. This procedure minimizes loss of the fish's protective coating of body slime.

Leaf netting

A sheet of lightweight plastic leaf netting prevents pond pollution caused by fallen leaves. In autumn, before leaves begin falling, stretch leaf netting over the pond. Select netting with openings in the mesh that are small enough to catch most of the leaves that would fall into your pond. Support the net above the water using 2×4s or beach balls. Then secure the edges with stakes or bricks. Deluxe netting kits include poles for creating a tent effect that allows leaves to roll off toward the pond edges.

▲ Keep a section of the pond ice-free in winter to allow fish to get adequate levels of oxygen.

Pond vacuums

Pond vacuums suck up debris from the pond bottom. The simplest type consists of an empty cylinder on an extended handle. It works like a siphon as debris-laden bottom water replaces air in the cylinder. A garden hose powers the venturi-type vacuum. It collects debris in a fine-mesh bag attached to its sweep head. As with a home vacuum cleaner, you can change sweep heads. Use a small one for fine debris or a large head to collect leaves. To remove debris covering the bottom of a drained pond, use a wet-dry shop vacuum.

Pond deicers

A floating deicer maintains a hole in the ice that forms on a pond in cold-winter regions, allowing oxygen to reach the water and the toxic gases that arise from decaying material to escape. Both actions are vital to the well-being and survival of your plants and fish.

Basically, an electric deicer is a heating element attached to a float. It's plugged into a 120-volt outdoor outlet with a GFCI. The deicer's thermostat turns on the heating element as the water temperature approaches freezing and turns it off as the surface water temperature rises above freezing, heating a small volume of water in its vicinity. Most deicers are 100 to 1,500 watts, the equivalent of 1 to 15 lightbulbs of 100 watts. Hang a 50-watt deicer on the side of an in-ground container garden of 50 gallons or less.

DEICER NOTES

Operating a pump or air stone (an aeration device that releases air bubbles through the water) when using a deicer causes currents, which move the warmed water away from the deicer and make it consume extra power to warm colder water. In addition, deicers emit a small, harmless charge into the water that might trip the circuit breaker if it's connected to a sensitive GFCI. In this event consult an electrician to determine if the GFCI outlet can be replaced with a less sensitive one.

POND EMERGENCY KIT

▲ Keep a few basic items on hand to prevent a minor problem from becoming a crisis.

Even the most meticulously maintained water garden will experience a crisis once in a while. Being able to diagnose and correct problems quickly when they arise can turn a potential disaster into a minor inconvenience. Having a few basic items stored together in a convenient spot can be a big help when an emergency does occur.

Water quality test kit: Buy the best kit you can; it's worth it. There's no other reliable way to tell if chemicals in your water have reached toxic levels. If you take readings as part of your regular maintenance schedule, it will be easy for you to detect a change that indicates a problem. If something seems to be wrong in your pond, a quick test of the water is your first step toward diagnosis.

Water treatments: Most common water-quality problems are caused by too much chlorine or ammonia. If you use public tap water to fill your pond, be sure to have chlorine remover on hand. An accidental tap water overfill can increase the chlorine in the water to a fatal level for fish. Too much ammonia in the water is a more complicated issue. Ammonia can build up in a pond for many reasons—the weather is hot, the filters aren't functioning, the pump is broken—that ultimately require long-term solutions. To reduce ammonia levels in an emergency, use commercially available liquids or "rocks."

Backup pump or aerator: There's nothing more important to your aquatic ecosystem than oxygen. When the pump shuts down, oxygen is quickly depleted from the water, and the fish come to the surface to gasp for air. A small backup pump, air stone, or even a fine mist from the garden hose will keep the water oxygenated until you can repair your main pump.

Liner patch kit: If you've made sure a dramatic drop in water level has not been caused by evaporation or a leak in the waterfall, it's time to locate the leak and affix a patch with glue or tape, available from water garden suppliers.
Prepare a temporary holding tank for fish as you wait for the water to stop draining so you can hunt for the crack or puncture.

Plastic wading pool: If the quick fixes don't work and you must empty your pond to correct a problem, you'll need one or more temporary holding pens for fish and plants. Buckets work but they don't hold much water. Garbage cans are too deep. A more effective solution is a child's shallow plastic wading pool, which can be filled and dechlorinated quickly.

WATER QUALITY CHECKLIST

All local water supplies contain some form of chemical disinfectant, usually chlorine or chloramines. (Chloramines also occur in water naturally.) These disinfectants may be present alone or in combination.

Technically, plants will not be harmed by these chemicals, but attendant wildlife (snails and frogs, for example) will. It's best to remove the disinfectants in a new pond, even if you don't plan to stock fish.

Before you introduce fish or plants to your garden pond, check with your local water supplier to see which disinfectants are present in your water. Then take the following steps to remove them.

■ Use a dechlorinator to remove chlorine, or let the water in your pond stand for 5 to 7 days (the chlorine will dissipate in this period).

■ Eliminate chloramines with a chloramine remover, which also takes out any chlorine present. You can purchase chloramine remover at a water garden supply house. The action of both dechlorinators and chloramine removers is almost immediate. You can introduce or return fish into the pond shortly after using either one.

Follow the previous steps when stocking new ponds and when refilling the pond with more than 10 to 20 percent of the water volume.

When topping off the pond (to replace evaporated water, for example), you don't need to treat tap water. However, you do need to follow these steps:

■ Run the hose into the bottom of the pond.

■ Add the water slowly, in a trickle, to avoid shocking the fish and to avoid attracting them to the activity of the water bubbles. (Do not use the hose to aerate ponds containing fish.)

■ Replace no more than 10 to 20 percent of the water at a time. Set a timer if necessary.

TROUBLESHOOTING

■ **The liner shows:** Make sure the pond is full. If that doesn't solve the problem, disassemble the edging and re-lay it to make it level with the water surface. Dig soil out from underneath the edge of flexible liner to lower the edging. If necessary, add additional edging material or stone, making sure it overlaps the edging and disguises the exposed liner. Position sprawling plants alongside the edge to conceal the liner. They will provide a cosmetic fix as well as protect the liner from UV rays.

■ **The water looks or smells funny:** Soil erosion or mud splashed into the pond by heavy rain can cause consistently muddy water. Check around the water feature, especially at its edging. Spread any eroding or rain-splashed soil with gravel or organic mulch. You can also plant a groundcover.

Bad smells from your pond mean that anaerobic bacteria (those that don't use oxygen) are too abundant. Add a waterfall or a pump (or increase pump volume) to increase aeration. Promptly remove dead or decaying plant matter and dead fish. Minimize fish feeding, and withhold food during hot weather (above 80°F). Keep the water feature topped off in warm weather so the water doesn't get murky. Finally, reevaluate your ecosystem. Adding filtering plants may help. In severe cases, a biological water filter may be the solution.

■ **The pond is leaking:** Pond repair kits are readily available. To repair a pond, drain it with a pump or siphon and locate the leak. Remove anything that might have punctured the liner, such as stones or sticks. Back the puncture or tear, if possible, with damp sand or pond underlayment. Then clean and dry the surface areas completely. Using a pond liner adhesive and following repair-kit instructions, spread a generously sized patch (at least 2 inches longer and wider than the leak) with adhesive and attach it. Let the patch dry before refilling the pond.

■ **The pump stopped:** With proper care, a high-quality water-garden pump should last for several years. To prolong pump life, make sure debris or algae will not tax its motor. Clean the prefilter or intake filter at least once a week during the spring and up to three times a week in summer and fall. Set the pump on a brick or flat stone, not directly on the pond bottom, where it will take in more silt. If algae clog the pump, clean the pump and use a pump protector device such as an inexpensive plastic mesh box or a more expensive stainless steel cage.

Then place it inside a black plastic basket. Running the pump without water will burn out the motor.

■ **The pond is full of muck:** You will need to remove fallen leaves almost daily so they don't have a chance to decay and pollute the water. If your pool or pond is located under a tree or regularly collects fallen leaves, consider stretching netting or a leaf tent over the pond to catch the leaves. Anchor the netting on the sides with bricks or stakes driven into the soil. Remove these netted leaves regularly so they don't shade the water.

If the leaves have sunk to the bottom, they can be removed by hand or with a soft plastic rake. For larger pools, especially those without many plants or fish, consider investing in a pool sweep, which attaches to a garden hose and uses water pressure to remove debris and silt from the pond bottom. A spa vacuum or pond vacuum will also work. All are available from water garden suppliers.

▼ **To cover the exposed edges of a flexible liner, you may need to place additional rocks or adjust the existing ones.**

PROJECTS

▲ Trace the area for your planned water feature with a garden hose or twine and observe it for a week or so to make sure you have chosen the best site.

◄ Choose a water garden project that fits the size of your yard as well as the time and funds you want to spend on it.

The most successful water gardens follow a plan and have a design that pulls together the entire project. You should integrate the plan and design with the contours and style of your home's landscape as well as with your lifestyle.

The best plan, therefore, will always reflect a balance of both practical and aesthetic elements. For example, the size and shape of your water garden should conform not only to the scale of your yard but also to the time and funds you can devote to its installation and maintenance.

If you have less than an hour each week to devote to caring for your pond, consider a small installation, even if you have a large backyard. Place it in an intimate corner of the yard to keep it in scale with its surroundings. Similarly, if your schedule allows you to enjoy your pond only in the evening and on weekends, you might want to have a "moon garden," with tropical water lilies and other night-blooming plants. Add lighting around the water feature to enhance your ability to enjoy the garden through the evening hours.

If your primary interest is attracting birds and butterflies, you need to include design features such as a sandy butterfly beach or a shallow area at the pond edge to serve as a birdbath. Include flowering plants such as swamp milkweed and purple coneflower around the water garden. These will serve as nectar and food sources for wildlife.

Families with young children might take comfort in the safety of a shallow bog garden with lotuses or a splashing fountain with no deep pools of water.

Gardeners who enjoy entertaining outdoors might choose to build a small, formal pool within a well-planted seating area. Others might create multiple ponds connected by streams and falls in a natural setting. Hobbyists may want to focus on features most compatible with fish.

Look through the projects that follow for inspiration and guidelines. Recreate the project in your own yard if it fits your needs. Or adapt the design to your site and interests before embarking on the project.

If you already enjoy gardening, the tools you keep on hand will be appropriate to begin many of the water garden projects on the following pages. Most are do-it-yourself designs that can be completed in a few hours to a few weekends. The rewards will last for years.

BOGS AND STREAMS

Natural bog

Instead of filling your bog with soil, use silica sand—the kind used in sandblasting or in pool filters. Avoid limestone-based sand. It is harmful to the plants because the lime forms compounds with other minerals in the sand, making nutrients unavailable.

For a natural bog you'll need to plant sphagnum moss, the best indicator of the health of a bog. If it is turning brown and having trouble growing, other bog plants won't grow either. If the moss is growing well, other bog plants will also flourish.

■ **Builder's notes:** First, place a few inches of premoistened, long-fiber, dried sphagnum moss on the surface of the soil. On top of that, place live sphagnum moss. You can use just the dry sphagnum moss, provided it has some green tips, to provide spores that will grow into live sphagnum moss. You may also find that additional sphagnum moss is likely to be attached to small carnivorous plants from the store.

Irrigate natural bogs with acid (pH 6) water low in minerals. Distilled water or rainwater are good sources to start the bog.

▲ **Keep visitors from getting too close to the water's edge with a bog between the pond and land.**

Bog at pond's edge

A bog can enhance the safety of your water garden. If you're fearful that visitors or children might slip and fall into the water, build the pond with solid edges to make it stable. Then add a bog as a buffer between visitors and open water.

You can include a bog regardless of the dimensions of your pond or stream. Along one edge of the water feature in the photo above, a bog provides ample room for marginal water plants. A bridge over the stream creates an excellent viewing platform. Large flat stones on the edge opposite the bog provide a stable area for visitors to walk up to the water.

■ **Builder's notes:** The bog planting pocket is roughly 2 to 3 feet wide, 6 to 10 inches deep, and about 6 to 10 inches above the water line at the edge farthest from the pond. Place pond underlayment and liner in this pocket, and hold them in position at the far edge of the pocket with fieldstone. Fill in the pocket with clay soil. The pocket's pondside edge is below the water line, so water filters into the pocket and keeps the soil moist.

▼ **A bog garden solves the problem of a low spot in the yard, eases the transition from pond edge to landscape, or simply provides a place to grow water-loving plants.**

Freestanding bog

The bog garden forms a natural transition between a wet area and dry land. This freestanding bog includes water-loving marginal plants that thrive in moist soil. Exotic plants add an unexpected element to the residential landscape. A bog provides an ideal opportunity to turn a poorly draining site into a beautiful asset.

■ **Builder's notes:** Excavate to 16 inches deep. Line the site with a 2-inch layer of sand topped with a flexible liner. Install a perforated PVC pipe along the bottom of the bog. Use an elbow fitting to extend one pipe vertically to just above an outside edge so that you can connect it to a hose to keep the soil saturated. Cover the bottom of the bog with a 3-inch layer of gravel topped with a landscape fabric weed barrier to keep soil out of the gravel. Then refill the bog

▲ **Water-loving cotton grass and irises create a natural transition from a freestanding bog to dry land.**

with excavated soil mixed with generous amounts of peat moss.

■ **Approximate size:** 10×15 feet
■ **Variations:** Make the bog a narrow strip, a small pocket adjacent to a pond or stream, or a sprawling wetland. Plant a bog garden in a large plastic tub sunk into the ground. Then fill it with a collection of carnivorous plants. Substitute a leaky hose for PVC pipe.

YOU WILL NEED

■ 1 EPDM rubber liner, 15×20 feet
■ Geotextile underlay (optional)
■ 12 feet of 1½-inch PVC pipe
■ Elbow fitting
■ Hose fitting
■ PVC sealant
■ 1 ton sand
■ 1 ton gravel
■ Rock for edging
■ 1 bale peat moss
■ Immersible containers (optional)
■ Plants: ligularia, taro, thalia, arrowhead, parrot's feather, rush, ludwigia, yellow iris

---

■ **BOG GARDEN PLAN**

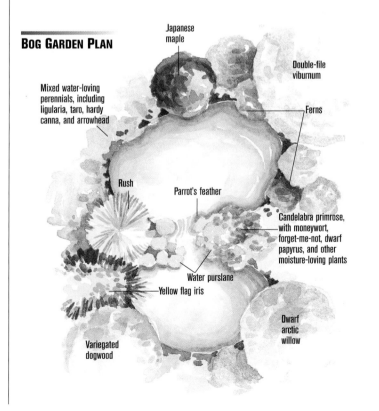

Japanese maple

Double-file viburnum

Mixed water-loving perennials, including ligularia, taro, hardy canna, and arrowhead

Ferns

Rush

Parrot's feather

Candelabra primrose, with moneywort, forget-me-not, dwarf papyrus, and other moisture-loving plants

Water purslane

Yellow flag iris

Variegated dogwood

Dwarf arctic willow

YOU WILL NEED

- 1 EPDM rubber liner, 5×45 feet
- 2 EPDM rubber liners, 10×15 feet
- Geotextile underlayment
- 2 tons sand
- 1 ton washed gravel
- 2 tons river rock
- 4,000 gph pump
- 70 feet of 2-inch PVC pipe; 30 feet of 1½-inch PVC pipe
- Fittings: one 2-inch PVC Y-fitting; two 2×1½-inch PVC reducers; 2 gate valves; PVC elbows, as needed; connector to pump (varies with pump)
- PVC glue
- UV clarifier (optional)

◀ **A stream attracts wildlife and offers visual interest all year long. Include a seating area nearby so you can relax and listen to the stream's natural bubbling music.**

Streams

Two streams become one as they rush to two ponds below. A small waterfall connects the ponds; another small waterfall splits the stream in two. The rushing water draws attention to its beauty and sound. A strategically placed, comfortable chair invites the visitor to linger. The feature attracts wildlife and offers year-round interest. Landscaping includes trees, shrubs, and perennials suitable for shade.

■ **Builder's notes:** Every stone is carefully selected and placed with consideration of how it affects the water's flow. Excavating the stream takes one day. Include some 10- to 12-inch deep pools. Digging the double pond takes another day. Use an algicide for a feature that includes no fish.

■ **Variations:** Use a simpler design, including one pool and a single stream. Aquatic plants, such as iris and pickerel rush, could be added to quiet nooks in the stream. Water lilies, submerged plants, and marginal plants could inhabit the two ponds. Divert one-third of the water to run through a UV clarifier to keep the water running clear.

STREAM PLAN

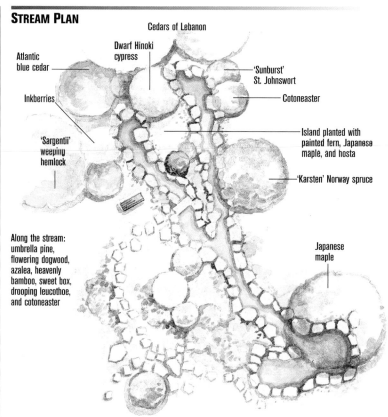

- Cedars of Lebanon
- Dwarf Hinoki cypress
- Atlantic blue cedar
- Inkberries
- 'Sargentii' weeping hemlock
- 'Sunburst' St. Johnswort
- Cotoneaster
- Island planted with painted fern, Japanese maple, and hosta
- 'Karsten' Norway spruce
- Along the stream: umbrella pine, flowering dogwood, azalea, heavenly bamboo, sweet box, drooping leucothoe, and cotoneaster
- Japanese maple

◀ After excavating the watercourse and placing the liner, position rocks and boulders along the path to create a natural appearance.

▼ The finished project is an enticing series of pools and rapids.

▲ Span a stream with a simple bridge to enjoy the site of moving water close up. Seating nearby takes advantage of the soothing sound of flowing water.

SPLIT FLOW

Building a waterfall or stream is like creating a moving sculpture. You can design it so the water rushes from one pool to the next, or you can shape it so the water bubbles gently over strategically placed rocks. Increase motion and visual interest in your waterfall or stream by splitting the flow of water. A split in the water adds an appealing dimension to a simple stream or falls.

A split flow creates two distinct water paths and offers unique views of one feature. A split flow in a stream can allow one watercourse to meander quietly along a curving route while the other jumps across stones and splashes marginal plants. If your water feature will traverse several levels down a slope, consider splitting the flow from one tier into two or three paths and then reuniting them at a lower tier before the water joins the pond below. Arrange rocks to narrow or widen each path as desired.

Before you put the liner down, plan for a split flow while sculpting the water's path with soil. To split the flow in a waterfall, choose an appropriate spot to install a wide tier where the split will start. Then make the next tier narrower where the two watercourses will be

reunited toward the edge of the falls. The water will move faster and produce more sound where the path narrows.

If your waterfall flows from a wide-lipped box, the first landing will be one solid flow. Split the flow by placing one medium- or large-size rock slightly off center on that tier, creating unequal paths for the water on either side. Position the rock near the edge of the falls. Group several smaller rocks around it to make its appearance look natural. Pitting the force of moving water against immobile rock heightens the drama of your waterfall.

If your waterfall flows from a hose at the top, you can immediately split the flow on the first tier with a Y connector. Attach short pieces of hose to the Y to aim the water in different directions. The size of your pump and the diameter of your hose determine the flow rate. To create a quieter water flow on one side of the split, add reducer fittings to that section of hose.

Watching water in motion is a captivating pastime. The more dynamic your design, the more you will enjoy the sights and sounds of your water feature.

CLAY POND

YOU WILL NEED

- ■ Bald cypress or other planks: 1 inch thick by 12 inches wide; thinner for curved sections
- ■ 30- to 42-inch-long pipes (iron water pipes)
- ■ Sledgehammer
- ■ Shovel
- ■ Marginal and aquatic plants

▲ A clay pond is the most natural type you can build. The wood plank walls don't show under water, and the pond-edge plantings blend into the surrounding landscape.

◄ Marginal plants such as pickerel weed take root in clay ponds.

A natural clay-sided pond has several distinct and desirable advantages if you have good clay soil in which to build one. First, the soil can stabilize an eroding bank while it keeps the area as natural as possible—no plastic rims or concrete sides to contend with. You can turn a much-used drainage ditch into an attractive asset rather than an eyesore by emptying it into a clay pond.

■ **A few pointers:** Use any lumber for the sides because it won't rot under water. If a nearby stream is the source of water, direct the water from it through a pipe to the pond to avoid any sediment buildup. Close off the pipe to drain the pond for cleanup.

■ **Set planks:** Dig out the shape. Lay the planks on edge and hammer the pipes 18 inches into the ground to hold the frame in place. Stack two planks in a section by a slope. For curved sections, soak thin planks in water overnight to soften them. Then bend them into a curve. Set them on top of thicker straight planks.

■ **Water:** Fill the pond with water. The planks will not show because they will be at least an inch below the surface. Bog plants should survive even if water seeps out—and it will, despite a packed clay bottom. To accommodate water lilies, floating plants, and fish, keep a garden hose nearby for topping off the pond.

SIMPLE LINED POND

A basic pond, adjustable to a large or small scheme that fits the site, provides an opportunity for diving into water gardening. This pond operates as a well-balanced system with neither a pump nor a filter. The design creates an informal pool that features both plants and still-water reflection. Add goldfish for even more enjoyment.

■ **Builder's notes:** Easy to construct and maintain, this classic water garden with a winding path to the house provides outstanding views from indoors. The pond's mortared-stone edging enables access for maintenance and encourages closer viewing. Only basic equipment is needed for this project.

■ **Approximate size:** 10×15 feet

■ **Variations:** Design a wildlife pond, including a shallow beach and a variety of plants attractive to wildlife. Create a hidden garden with mysterious appeal that offers a quiet retreat in an enclosed, out-of-the-way spot. The path could be traded for a bermed area with a waterfall. Add a stream, an adjacent paved entertainment area, or a fountain. Alternative building materials include preformed liner; cut stone, concrete pavers, or wood decking for edging; and endless variations of plants.

▲ **No pump or filter is needed for this informal pool. Aquatic plants, goldfish, and snails keep it in balance.**

YOU WILL NEED

■ 1 rubber pond liner, 15×20 feet
■ 1 geotextile underlayment
■ 1 to 1½ tons sand
■ 5 bags ready-mix mortar
■ 1 ton washed gravel
■ 1½ tons river rock
■ 3 potted water lilies
■ 10 potted marginal plants, such as cardinal flower, cattail, papyrus, and rush
■ 36 bunches submerged plants, such as fanwort and willow moss
■ 20 black Japanese snails
■ 6 goldfish

SIMPLE LINED POND PLAN

Mixed perennials: scotch bells, blue lobelia, hen-and-chicks, soapwort, ornamental grass, and rose campion

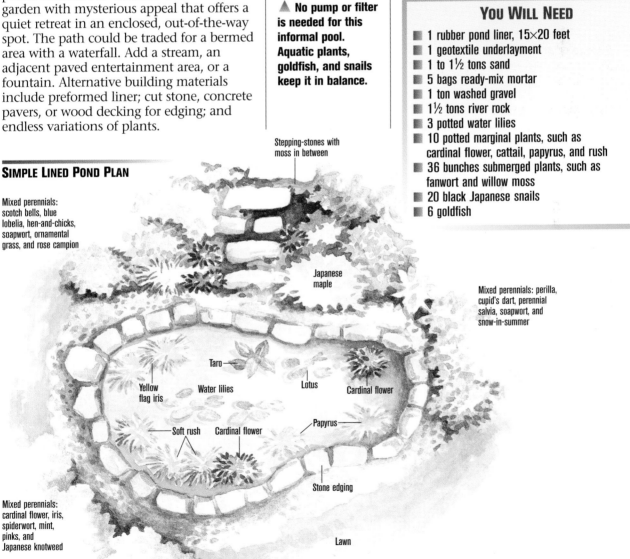

Stepping-stones with moss in between

Japanese maple

Mixed perennials: perilla, cupid's dart, perennial salvia, soapwort, and snow-in-summer

Taro

Lotus

Cardinal flower

Yellow flag iris

Water lilies

Papyrus

Soft rush

Cardinal flower

Stone edging

Mixed perennials: cardinal flower, iris, spiderwort, mint, pinks, and Japanese knotweed

Lawn

POND WITH FLEXIBLE LINER

▲ Select a water garden site in full sun.

1. Select a site: Select a site that is away from deciduous trees so you won't be constantly cleaning out fallen flowers in spring and leaves in autumn—a wise precaution no matter what material you are using for your water garden. Even though you will pad the ground underneath the pond before laying down the liner, avoid rocky areas. Rocks can puncture the liner.

Choose a location in direct sun or with midday light shade if you live in warmer zones. Most water plants grow best with at least 6 hours of sun daily. Avoid placing the pond at the lowest point in your yard. Water runoff from heavy rains can cause problems in ponds on low sites.

2. Outline: Decide on the shape of the pond. (Make a preliminary drawing on paper, indicating the pond's relationship to other areas in the yard.) Use a garden hose, lime, landscape paint, or flour to outline curved sections. If your design includes straight edges, stretch a length of string between stakes for those sections.

Look at the pond's shape and location from a distance such as the patio, the deck, or even inside the house. This gives you a feeling for how the finished project will look. Rearrange the outline until you have a shape you like.

ou have many more options for shapes and sizes when you build a pond with a flexible liner, but it does take planning and some additional building time. Although you can make any shape you want, simple shapes are the easiest to excavate and set up. It is easier to excavate for a pond with a flexible liner than one with a rigid, preformed liner.

▲ **Flexible liners make building a water garden easy, allowing you to create a simple pond in almost any shape. Add a small circulating fountain or some garden sculpture to complete the scene.**

YOU WILL NEED
- Flexible liner, 20 to 45 mil thick
- Garden hose or lime
- String and stakes
- Shovel, carpenter's level
- 2×4 (for leveling)
- Builder's sand
- Geotextile fabric or other underlayment
- Stones, pavers
- Pump-and-fountain kit
- Deep-water plants such as tropical water lily
- Floating plants such as water lettuce
- Marginal plants such as yellow flag iris

3. Dig: Excavate the hole at least 18 inches deep, preferably with the assistance of several helpers. Slope the sides and keep the bottom flat. At one end, or along one side, dig a 1-foot-wide terrace 8 to 12 inches deep to hold pots of marginal plants. If you plan to edge the pond with flat stones or bricks, dig a ledge 3 to 4 inches deep for that purpose.

4. Level: Lay a 2×4 across the pond and set a carpenter's level on it to check that the edge is the same height all around. Keeping the edge level will prevent the liner from showing when you have filled the pond.

If the pond is too wide for the 2×4, attach a line level to a length of string. Pull the string taut at different points across the length and width of the excavation.

Add or remove soil until the edge is level. Then lower a small section of the edge by ½ inch to allow overflow to drain off during heavy rains.

5. Underlayment: Spread 2 inches of sand over the bottom of the excavation before putting down the underlayment.

Cover the bottom and sides of the pond with an underlayment of newspapers spread in full sections, old carpet, or geotextile fabric to protect the liner from protruding rocks and roots.

6. Liner: To figure out the liner size you need, measure the pond length and width. Then add twice the depth plus 2 feet all around to allow for overlap. Move the liner gently into place in the excavation. Leave wrinkles for slack along the curves. Temporarily anchor the edge of the liner with stones.

Slowly fill the pond with water and smooth the liner as needed. The wrinkles will not show when the pond is full.

▶ **Outline the pond shape with flour, lime, or string.**

▼ **A site away from tree roots will make it easier to dig.**

◀ **Make sure the edges are level all around so that no water seeps out after you fill the pond.**

▼ **A garden hose is a convenient way to fill the pond.**

▲ **Protect the liner from sharp rocks and roots by covering the excavated area with layers of carpet, newspaper, or geotextile fabric before you put the liner in position.**

▶ Secure the edge of the pond liner with flat stones fit together as securely as possible.

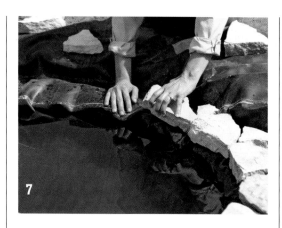

▲ When all the stones are in place and the liner is secure, trim all but 1 foot off the excess.

7. Edging: Remove the stones you used to hold the liner in place temporarily. Set flat stones around the rim of the pond on the 3-inch-deep ledge and secure the edge of the liner under them.

Abut any irregularly shaped stones as if they were pieces of a puzzle. They should form a fairly level first course (layer). Use pavers, bricks, flagstones, or cut stones to build the edge. If you want, position some of the pavers or stones so they overhang the rim of the pond slightly.

8. Trim: Using sharp scissors, trim the liner to within 1 foot of the edge of the first course of stones.

9. Second course: Set a second course of stones on top of the first, pulling the liner securely under the stones as you lay them. Center each stone over the joint of a stone in the first course. Double edging ensures that the liner will not slip.

The liner is invisible from the pond side. To hide it on the exterior side, use edging plants. Take your time in deciding on the plants to place around the pond. Good choices to consider are daylilies, hostas, and yellow or purple coneflowers.

10. Additions: If you want, add one or more courses of stones to create a decorative edging, which will have the appearance of a drystack stone wall. This raised wall

is perfect for holding a larger fountain or a small spitter (a decorative object that sprays water into the pond). Plan for that before you place the second course of stones. Leave a small opening through which to guide the tube from the recirculating pump to the fountain.

11. Pump: If you include a pump and fountain in the pond, rest it on the bottom of the pond—in the center, off to one side, or near one end. Bring a small pump closer to the surface by putting it on bricks or cinder blocks. (Scrub new cinder or concrete blocks with a stiff brush dipped in a solution of 1 part vinegar and 3 parts water; then rinse.) Keep the fountain away from water lilies, which prefer still water.

12. Plant: Use a dechlorinating product to treat the water. Then set in plants.

Set deep-water plants, such as water lilies, at 18-24 inches deep. Place the pots on bricks or concrete blocks if necessary.

Place marginal plants, such as irises, papyrus, and cattails, in pots on the terrace created as you dug the pond (see pages 102–103). Wait for a week or two for the water to stabilize before adding fish.

▶ Center the stones in the second layer over the joints of the stones in the first layer, pulling the liner tightly between the layers.

▲ Add more layers of stones for a drystack edging effect. You can also create a raised wall at one end to hold a fountain or other ornament.

POND WITH RIGID LINER

▲ Use a preformed liner to create a partially aboveground pool. Finish the outside walls and lip with wood decking or stones.

A pond with a rigid liner is like a large sunken container, with subtle differences. A preformed pond offers more space for plants but takes more time to dig. Although you can work to approximate the exterior shape, you need to be more exact with the length, width, and placement of the interior shelf.

■ **Builder's notes:** Turn the preformed liner upside down on the pond site and trace around its perimeter with lime, spray paint, or flour. Then turn the liner right side up and set it nearby so you can refer to its interior contours as you dig. Excavating the hole will be easier if you avoid rocky areas and large tree roots. Once you've placed the liner, fill it with water, and backfill around it with sand.

Camouflage the rim of the liner by laying rocks and flat stones on it. Place some so they overhang the water for a natural look. Use some of the flat stones as shelves for potted flowering and foliage plants.

YOU WILL NEED

- Preformed pond liner
- Lime, paint, or flour
- Stakes
- Shovel
- Sand
- Pump
- Assorted rocks and flat stones
- Potted plants
- Floating plants

▲ Camouflage the liner rim with plants and rocks. Exposed liner looks out of place in an otherwise natural environment.

CONCRETE POND

Long before preformed and flexible liners came into existence, concrete was the material of choice for ponds. It is inexpensive and long-lasting if you take precautions and some extra care in building and maintaining the concrete.

■ **Dig and prepare:** Decide on the shape of the pond, using a garden hose or rope to outline it. Remember to consider the thickness of the concrete and add about 6 inches all around. Outline the shape with lime, flour, or spray paint. Excavate the soil, digging to the depth you want plus 6 inches for the concrete. Slope the sides to about a 20-degree angle. Dig a shelf for edge plants, if desired. Compact the earth on the bottom and especially on the sides. Make sure the top edges of the pond are level. If you include a pump and fountain, decide where to place the electrical cord and water-return line.

■ **Reinforce:** Contour concrete reinforcing mesh in the hole. About 12 inches above the bottom, drive in metal stakes, leaving

▲ A pond with sloping sides is easier to build than one with straight sides, which requires the use of wooden forms. Build the pond in mild, dry weather so that the concrete will cure properly.

▲ Stone edging at the pond's lip and on the inside walls disguises the construction and creates pockets for water spillways.

6 inches protruding, to hold the mesh. The stakes guide you in keeping the concrete a uniform 6 inches thick on all surfaces.

■ **Pour:** Pour the ready-mix concrete into one part of the pool at a time (concrete sets up quickly) and pack it into the mesh with a trowel. When you reach 6-inch thickness, pull out the stakes or drive them into the ground and fill the stake holes with concrete. Pour the next portion. Dampen the concrete periodically to retard the curing process.

■ **Protect:** After you have poured all of the concrete and smoothed its surface with the trowel, cover the pond with a sheet of polyethylene, holding it in place with a few strategically placed bricks. The polyethylene slows the curing process and keeps rain out of the pool until the concrete has completely hardened. Concrete that has cured slowly is stronger than concrete that has cured quickly in hot weather.

YOU WILL NEED

- Garden hose or rope; lime, flour, or paint
- Shovel and carpenter's level
- Masonry trowel and mortar
- Ready-mix concrete
- Concrete reinforcing mesh
- Metal stakes
- Polyethylene sheets
- Bricks, pavers, or cut stones
- Pipe or conduit
- Stiff-bristle brush
- Pool paint sealant or plaster

Curing: The concrete will take a week to cure completely. Remove a 4- to 12-inch area of sod surrounding the pool to make room for a rim. Then mortar a coping of brick, pavers, or cut stone around the edge to provide the lip. Place a length of pipe under the section closest to the GFCI electrical outlet when you mortar so you have housing for the wiring of a recirculating pump. Use a level to make sure all the coping is even.

Finishing: Fill the pool with water. Let the water stand at least 24 hours and then drain. Scour the concrete with a stiff-bristle brush to remove cement residue and rinse well. Cleaning prevents concrete from leaching into the water and making it a cloudy, undesirable environment for fish or plants. Because concrete is porous, seal the surface with pool paint or plaster made from white marble powder and cement.

▶ Concrete ponds cover a range of styles, from traditional to naturalistic. A gently bubbling fountain and lily pads create a classic look.

▲ Blend the pond into its natural surroundings by planting low-growing evergreens or perennial groundcovers that will spread among randomly placed rocks.

▲ Add slate or other flat stones to create seating around the rim of an aboveground concrete pool. Before filling, clean and seal the pool interior so that the water stays clear.

Runnel

A runnel is a small channel through which water flows. It connects two ponds or stands alone as a unique water feature. You can make it as long or short and as high or low as you want. The only limiting factor is the hose length for the recirculating pump. Runnels provide a rather formal look to landscape design. They look good in courtyards, on terraces, and along entry walks. Building a runnel is easiest if done before installing other hardscaping, although you can add one to an existing walkway.

■ **Measure stones:** Use pieces of slate or concrete pavers 1 inch thick by 8 inches wide for the sides and bottom of the runnel. The pieces can be any length. You can have the stone cut to fit the exact dimensions you want for the runnel or build it based on the size of the stones. Have at least eight pieces of stone cut in half lengthwise.

■ **Dig trench:** Dig a trench at least 10 inches deep and 12 inches wide. Use a string tied between two stakes to keep the line straight. Add 2 inches of fine gravel to the bottom of the trench.

■ **Lay stones:** Lay stones flat on the gravel to form the bottom of the runnel. Apply masonry epoxy between all joints. Use a rubber mallet to tap the stones into place. Check that each stone is level. To make the sides, start with a half-piece of stone so the joints of the bottom pieces don't overlap with those of the side pieces. Set the stones

▲ **Add the sound of trickling water to a terrace or courtyard with a runnel. A recirculating pump keeps the water flowing.**

on edge, flush with the outside edge of the bottom piece. Cap one end with a half-piece. Build a 16-inch-square return box for the pump at the other end.

■ **Install pump:** Leave a ½-inch gap between two of the edging stones for the pump cord. Once all stone is in place, use silicone caulk to seal joints that will be under water. Place the pump in the return box and plug it in. Depending on the size of the pump, you may want to attach a return line (a hose for the water to run in) to the pump. Placed at the far end of the runnel, it will move the water the entire length of the feature.

Seasonal care

Although the pump will recirculate water, you may need to replenish the water supply occasionally. Unplug the pump in autumn in zones where winter temperatures fall below freezing.

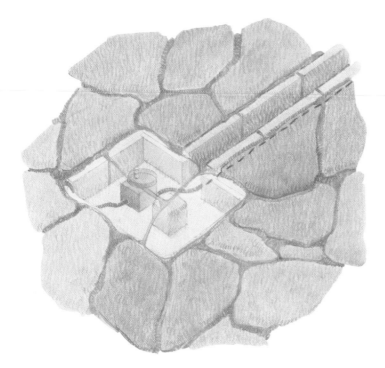

YOU WILL NEED	
■ Slate or concrete	■ Rubber mallet
■ Pavers, 1×8 inches	■ Carpenter's level
× any length	■ Silicone caulk
■ Shovel	■ Fine gravel
■ Stakes and string	■ Submersible pump
■ Masonry epoxy	■ Hose

RAISED POND WITH WATERFALL

Situated on a patio next to a Victorian-style home, this striking two-level pond takes a contemporary approach to the classical lines of a formal design. Besides providing the customary attraction of sparkling water, the refreshing waterfall music camouflages traffic noise and soothes the owners to sleep at night. Located in a frequently used area near the house, the raised pond provides hours of enjoyment while owners are dining or entertaining on the patio. The stone-capped walls provide seating and protect against an accidental plunge.

Builder's notes: The centerpieces of the pond include a fountain and a waterfall. A 3-foot-wide sheet of water spills 18 inches into the lower pond and recirculates to the

▲ **A waterfall enhances the design of an aboveground formal pond by adding music and movement to the patio or yard.**

upper pool. The feature's stacked-fieldstone veneer and flagstone edging repeat building materials used to construct the nearby walls, steps, walkways, and patio. Plantings include submerged oxygenators, water lilies, irises, and rushes. Whimsical statuary adds charm.

Approximate size: 15×15 feet

Variations: The project could be located at the edge of a deck. Or make the pond a different shape lined and edged with concrete, tile veneer, or brick edging.

YOU WILL NEED

- 1 EPDM rubber liner, 20×20 feet
- 1 EPDM rubber liner, 10×15 feet
- 70 feet flagstone
- 3 tons fieldstone
- 5 hardy water lilies
- 15 irises
- 6 rushes
- 4 decorative stone or metal frogs
- 12 comet goldfish
- 50 bunches submerged plants
- 50 black Japanese snails
- Submersible pump for the waterfall
- Submersible pump for the piped statuary
- 2 piped ornamental statuary pieces

RAISED POND WITH WATERFALL PLAN

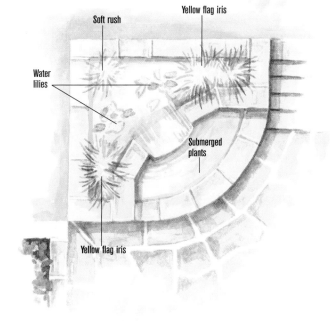

Soft rush

Yellow flag iris

Water lilies

Submerged plants

Yellow flag iris

POND WITH WATERFALL

A natural, gentle slope in the landscape makes an ideal setting for a watercourse. Take advantage of the change in elevation to join two or more ponds with a waterfall in between. In this project, waterfalls link three stone-lined ponds. Careful planting around and among the rocks blends the watercourse with the landscape.

■ **Builder's notes:** Perennials and upright evergreens surround the feature, linking it naturally to the site. Large, flat stones provide spillways for the waterfalls and seating along the edge of the pools.

■ **Approximate size:** About 20×60 feet overall (two pools 15×15 feet; one 20×20 feet; two waterfalls)

■ **Variations:** The feature could include two or three ponds with linking waterfalls or a stream with cascading ponds. Make small or narrow bogs along the ponds to transition to surrounding plantings. Extend the planting materials into the ponds, including water lilies and other aquatic plants. Add fish to the lower pond.

▲ Splashing water makes a garden irresistible to all kinds of visitors, including birds and other wildlife.

▲ Use a naturally sloping property to your advantage by building a series of cascading pools highlighted by a waterfall. Colorful marginal and perennial plants along the watercourse add even more appeal.

YOU WILL NEED

■ 2 EPDM rubber liners, 20×20 feet
■ 1 EPDM rubber liner, 25×25 feet
■ Geotextile fabric
■ 2 to 3 tons sand
■ 40-pound bag of gravel (for filling pots)
■ 4 tons rock
■ 55 feet PVC pipe or kink-free tubing
■ Fittings: Ls, Ys, and clamps
■ Black urethane foam
■ 50 bunches of submerged plants
■ Yellow flag irises
■ 50 black Japanese snails
■ 8 comet goldfish
■ 2,000–4,000 gph submersible pump
■ Biological filter

POND WITH WATERFALL PLAN

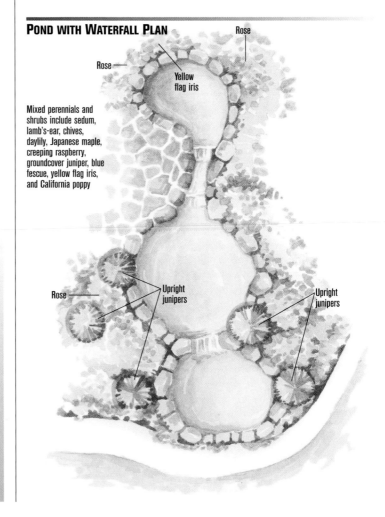

Mixed perennials and shrubs include sedum, lamb's-ear, chives, daylily, Japanese maple, creeping raspberry, groundcover juniper, blue fescue, yellow flag iris, and California poppy

Rose

Rose

Yellow flag iris

Rose

Upright junipers

Upright junipers

STEPPING-STONES

Easier maintenance and increased viewing pleasure are the practical and aesthetic reasons for installing stepping-stones. Remember two things for safety: Use stones with a rough surface so they will not be slippery when wet, and securely fasten the stones to a solid base.

It is easier to install stepping-stones in a pond without water than a filled one. Plan for and construct them as you build the pond. Drain water from an existing pond before starting.

Step placement: Be aware of changes in levels on the bottom of the pond and any challenges they may pose. For safety and aesthetics, it is important that you must have a level walking surface.

Water surface: When you have an idea of approximately where you want the stones, drive a stake outside the pond liner on either side of an imaginary line passing through the center of where the steps will be. Run twine between the stakes and use a line level to adjust the twine so it is even with where the surface of the water will be.

Spacing: Lay the pavers on a driveway following the configuration laid out above. Position them so you can walk across them comfortably. Sketch the layout on paper, marking all dimensions.

Foundation: Place a scrap of carpet or rigid builder's insulation board where each stepping-stone will be. With the sketch as a guide, stack the large concrete blocks on

▲ **Rough-surface stones provide sure footing when wet. Use mortar to attach each one to a solid, level support below.**

their sides on top of the carpet until they are ½ inch below the string. (The half inch allows for the mortar that will be between each of the concrete blocks and the pavers.) You may need to use narrower capstones to get the exact height. Set the pavers in place.

Building: Mix several batches of mortar. Take apart the piers. Then reassemble them using ½ inch of mortar between blocks all the way up to and including the stepping-stones. Allow the mortar to set for 3 days. Cover everything with a tarp if it rains.

YOU WILL NEED

- Line level, stakes, and twine
- Nonskid pavers, at least 2 inches thick and 18 inches wide
- Concrete blocks
- Carpet or rigid builder's insulation board
- 24×24-inch capstones (if needed)
- Premixed mortar

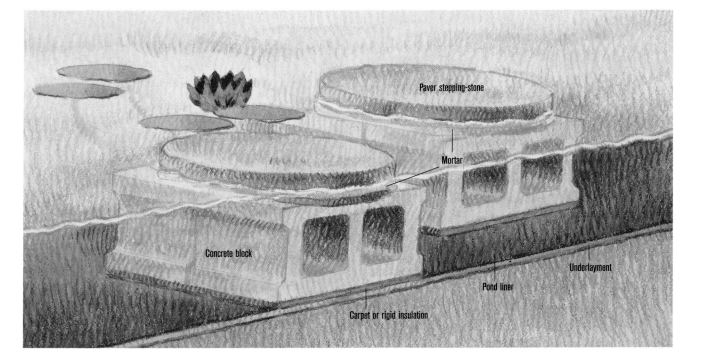

Paver stepping-stone

Mortar

Concrete block

Pond liner

Underlayment

Carpet or rigid insulation

DRY CREEK

YOU WILL NEED

- Rope or garden hose
- Shovel
- Rototiller (optional)
- Permeable landscape fabric
- River stones, rough rocks, pebbles
- Boulders
- Flat stones (stepping-stones)

Utilize plants that live naturally beside a real stream such as irises, cardinal flowers, hostas, and astilbes. Summer some of your houseplants, such as clivia and orchids, outdoors in the shelter of a fenced dry-creek garden. They will appreciate the heat reflected from the stones and the shelter from the wind and hot sun.

1. Design and dig: Using rope or a garden hose, lay out the contours of the stream in a meandering, casual style. Vary the width.

Sometimes just the impression of a stream is all that's needed. Many people have unused areas in the yard because these spaces do not seem to lend themselves to a pretty garden design. The most common unused spaces include a wet expanse of ground at the rear of the property and a side yard. Both places present an opportunity to take advantage of design challenges in the landscape.

A dry streambed can function as a drainage ditch for the wet area, while its beauty masks the utilitarian aspect. A well-planted dry creek can even filter obtrusive street noises from outside the yard. A winding trail of polished or rough stones bordered by hedges and beds of colorful annuals and perennials invites visitors to take a relaxing stroll.

Side yards and rear property lines often include fences, which make excellent backdrops for plantings. The addition of a dry creek is a perfect opportunity for designing a special, private garden retreat.

A few pointers: To save money, you can put in an underlayment of ordinary rough stones and use polished river stones for the top layer only. The subdued gray of the river stones, above left, beautifully offsets the greens and floral hues of the plants.

▲ A dry streambed provides a peaceful path through the garden in sunny weather and a convenient drainage ditch when it rains.

▶ Rototill the creek bed to make it easier to excavate.

▶ Dig the bed so that it runs slightly downhill, to carry water away when it rains.

To make digging easier, you can rototill the creek bed first. If the stream is very large, you may want to rent an earth-moving tractor to cut the initial swath. Use the excavated soil to mound a creek bank or to fill low spots elsewhere on your property. Dig the bed to a depth of 6 to 8 inches. Even on flat property, the bed should run slightly downhill to carry a stream of water during heavy rains.

2. Shape: It's visually interesting to have some straight, deep sides and some curved sides. Shape and tamp the sides and the bottom. They do not need to be perfectly smooth. Remove twigs, roots, stones, and other objects that might puncture the landscape fabric. Remove weeds and plants. Chop through large roots with an ax.

3. Lay fabric: Working on a still day, spread at least two layers of landscape fabric, such as permeable polypropylene fabric. With two layers, your dry creek will last a long time, eliminating the need to remove the covering rock and replace the fabric if it wears out. If you want the creek to carry water, use solid plastic sheeting. Place stones to secure the fabric. Smooth out each layer and overlap the bed edges.

4. Stonescape: Select stones in scale with the size of the stream. Smooth river rocks give the illusion of a more active creek. Rough stones give the impression that the creek has been dry for quite a while. Use a depth of 4 to 6 inches along the base of the stream. Mound the stones 6 to 8 inches deep along the edges to meet the banks. Place stepping-stones or add another point of interest, such as a waterfall made of stacked stones.

5. Anchor: Use boulders to anchor the landscape fabric that drapes up the sides and over the bank. Fill in with smaller boulders and river rocks to hide the fabric. Add more stones to the base of the creek and up the sides.

6. Landscape: Create a natural look along the stream edges, keeping them a little rough and irregular. Bury larger stones at least half their height in the soil rather than laying them directly on top of the soil. Soften the edges of the creek with groundcovers and perennials that will spread but not root in the stream itself. If some do, prune them occasionally to keep them overhanging instead of invading. Plant a few evergreen shrubs and dwarf trees along the creek and in beds nearby. You can also install a stepping-stone bridge or a raised wooden bridge.

◄ Remove any rocks or other sharp objects that might puncture the landscape fabric, then position the fabric in the bed of the creek.

◄ Fill in the bed of the dry creek with stones of nearly uniform size.

◄ Disguise the edges of the creek with larger stones and boulders.

▼ A dry creek with a curving shape is natural-looking and pleasing to the eye.

SWIMMING POOL TO POND CONVERSION

▲ **A naturalistic arrangement of boulders and shrubs transforms an old swimming pool into a new oasis.**

Do you have an unused swimming pool on your property that's just gathering leaves? Rather than backfilling it, you can easily transform it into a large water garden.

Your pool may be made of gunite and reinforced steel, but even if it's a liner pool or in need of replastering and retiling, you can still convert it to a koi pond or other waterscape. Most of the hard work is already done. The hole is dug, the dirt has been hauled away, and the plumbing and electrical are in place. A design idea and the energy for a bit of cleanup and mechanical modification are all you need.

■ **Cleaning:** A chief concern in converting a swimming pool to a working water feature is the removal of chemicals and residues from the surfaces. Pool chemicals such as cyanuric acid and conditioner, chlorine, and bromine are general biocides that kill aquatic life. Remove chemicals completely.

You can do this with a procedure called acid/bleach washing, used in both swimming pool and ornamental aquatics maintenance. Drain the system and apply a water-diluted solution (about 10 percent muriatic acid) to the basin, plumbing, and mechanical surfaces (making sure to remove filter cartridges first). Then rinse and drain two more times.

Wear rubber gloves, old long-sleeved shirts and slacks, and eye protection. Once you've tackled this cleaning, it will seem simple and straightforward. Basin re-coating, plastering, and retiling will probably not be necessary as the coating

from algae in the pond will eventually hide any flaws. Be careful when walking in the pond for maintenance and other tasks as the algae makes surfaces slippery.

■ **Circulation and aeration:** Pump size and installation depend on what you want in your pond. For full-blown koi systems, the pump needs to run continuously. The pumping mechanisms installed for the swimming pool may not be the best available or most appropriate technology to use with your conversion. Most fully rated swimming pool pumps are designed to produce relatively high volume at high pressure. To protect aquatic life as well as save on electric costs, you will want some volume at not much pressure for your pond. Do your homework here, as there are good choices in fractional and multiple horsepower pumps for ponds that can be retrofitted to the existing pool plumbing. Compare power curves, water moved per kilowatt consumed, and service factors because the pump operation will probably be your greatest ongoing expense.

On the other hand, if you will operate your waterfall only when guests visit or if you want only a reflecting pond or a heavily planted water garden, your current pump may work operated manually as needed or timed automatically for a few minutes to a few hours daily.

For koi and other vigorous oxygen users, you may need to turn the water over frequently, whereas ponds with only plants need far less circulation. Generally, you can continue to use the main drain on the bottom of the pool as the pump's principal intake, rather than supplying another mid-depth intake. If you circulate your water daily and regularly remove sludge and leaves, you can avoid difficulties with stagnant water or stratification in your system. If you live in an area where freezing is a concern, consider deicing mechanisms, surface agitation, air stones, or the use of a small submersible pump to keep your water moving in cold weather.

Filtration: Swimming pool filters remove small amounts of debris from the water. Biological ponds call for extraction of larger quantities of larger matter. If your pond does not collect many leaves and has adequate biofiltration from aquatic plants, you may be able to remove the existing swimming pool filter media (diatomaceous earth sleeves, cartridges, or sand) and instead use plastic biomedia, ceramics, fused glass beads, or batting material.

A filter designed specifically for ponds is definitely required for koi ponds and other more serious projects. Construct a large container inside a new waterfall, or use an in-line series of plastic troughs. Even in-pond filters will work. Plan them carefully to expedite maintenance tasks.

Retrofitting: Your conversion may need new plumbing for intakes or discharges, such as waterfalls, to improve circulation or to allow for the passage of more water without resistance. If so, use schedule 40 PVC pipe and fittings. Copper pipe already in place is safe for your aquatic animals. Because of its patina, any copper ion released will be an insoluble solid.

If your pool has a heater, you can leave it and its plumbing intact. Otherwise, remove or retrofit them to lessen pumped-water drag. If you decide to retrofit your existing pump's plumbing, cut in barbed intake and discharge fittings on Ts or Ys and valves on the new pump's intake and discharge lines. These can be useful in regular vacuuming maintenance and occasional large water changes, allowing you to pull out the water and place the waste elsewhere.

Skimmer intakes can be problematic in pool-to-pond conversions. These areas can trap excess floating matter and even fish. Screen the skimmers with sturdy plastic mesh to prevent a tragedy.

Maintain your new pond the same as you would any other biological pond of irregular size and shape. Fish feeding, plant potting, re-potting, and fertilization will follow the same schedules.

◀ Swimming pool chemicals such as chlorine and bromine are powerful biocides that can harm fish and other aquatic life. The most important step in this project is to clean any such residue from all pool surfaces with an acid/bleach washing and several rinses.

◀ A swimming pool pump is too powerful for most water gardens, especially if your pond includes fish. Install a timer to run it for short periods as needed, or replace it with a pump designed to move less water at lower pressure.

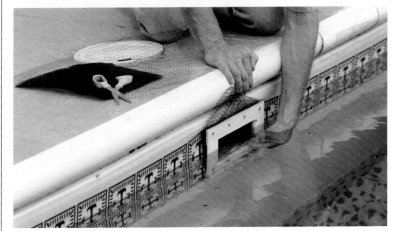

▲ The contents of a biological pond may overwhelm a swimming pool filter. Cover the skimmer intakes with sturdy plastic mesh to keep fish and floating plants from being pulled in. Add a fish filter.

BRIDGES

YOU WILL NEED

- Gravel (for footings)
- Cement mix (for footings)
- Lumber
- Rustproof decking screws
- Post-hole digger or shovel (for footings)
- Level and string level
- Circular saw
- Drill/power screwdriver

▲ An arched bridge with handrails allows visitors to cross a wide pond or stream without fear of falling in.

A bridge invites you to view your water feature from a unique vantage point. Observing your pond from overhead provides an opportunity for you to immerse yourself in its aquatic life in a new way. A bridge will keep you from also becoming physically immersed.

Spanning your pond with a bridge is not a complex project. You can even build the bridge over a small pond without footings if you have a stable surface on each bank and anchor the bridge to the ground with stakes.

■ **Building:** For a bridge spanning 8 feet or more, build 2 footings 2 feet apart on each bank. Dig the holes for your footings below the frost line. Fill the bottom of each hole with 2 inches of gravel. Set a treated 4x4 or 3-inch round post into the hole. Then scoop concrete mix into the hole. Use a torpedo level to make sure your posts are plumb. Use a string level to make sure your posts are level with one another. You may need to make a brace out of scrap wood to keep the posts straight until the concrete sets up. Leave the project overnight for the concrete to dry.

After your footings are set, bridge the gap across your pond with a single span of wood planks set on edge. A 2×6 will safely span 6 feet, a 2×8 will safely span 9 to

10 feet, and a 2×10 will safely span 12 feet. It will take two planks spanning the water to build your bridge's foundation, one connecting each pair of footings. Connect the planks with 1×2, 2×2, or 2×4 cross braces underneath, spacing the braces 2 feet apart. Finally, attach the 2×4 or 2×6 treads to the planks using 1 or 2 rustproof decking screws at each end. Three-foot-wide treads will help people crossing your bridge feel comfortable and secure. Leave a ¼- to ½-inch gap between the treads to allow for swelling and drainage.

For a gently arching bridge, the process is the same except for the two cross braces. Use a wide plank such as a 2×12 and draw an arc on it. The cross planks must be as thick as the span planks. For example, an arch plank cut from a 2×12 to span 9 feet must be no narrower than a 2×8. Cut out your first arc and use it to trace the same pattern on another 2×12. Arched bridges are self-reinforcing and are actually stronger than flat bridges.

▲ Attach sturdy bamboo poles between round posts to create a low guardrail that blends in with naturalized surroundings.

▼ Even a short span adds a unique point from which to observe the fish below.

▲ Decorative newel caps add an elegant touch to a simple plank and curved rail bridge.

▼ A flat pier supported by concrete pilings offers an unusual vantage point for viewing aquatic life.

▲ Painted guardrails along a simple span accent colors in the landscape.

Bridge handrail

A bridge railing can give garden visitors a feeling of security as they enjoy the aquascape below. You can easily construct a handrail for your bridge.

The simplest design is four posts set into the banks and strung with sturdy rope. This design works well on flat bridges that span only a short distance.

For bridges spanning more than 5 feet or for arched bridges, a wooden handrail bolted to the bridge offers both security and attractive style. You can make the posts with 2×4 or 4×4 lumber. A 4×4 post must be notched with a 2-inch cutout 6 inches up from the base where it will bolt to the bridge.

Trim off a bridge tread so the post will bolt directly to the bridge's support plank. Pre-drill the holes and use 5-inch rustproof lag bolts with washers to attach the post to the plank. First, place posts at both ends of the bridge. Then divide the distance between them into equal lengths to determine where to place the interior posts. Space the posts every 3 to 6 feet along the

▶ **Decorative handrails link the bridge style to the garden design and also offer safety.**

▼ **If the water is shallow and child safety is not a concern, you may prefer to span your water garden with wide planks and omit the handrail.**

bridge based on what looks attractive and proportionate for the span.

After the posts are securely attached, cut 2×4s to length for the railings. Attach the railings between the posts with rustproof screws drilled in at an angle on the undersides.

A second 2×4 rail installed 12 inches below the top one is a quick finish. Alternatively, install the second 2×4 rail four to six inches above the bridge treads and add 1×1 deck rail spindles between the two rails. You can top off the 4×4 posts with finials.

HINT

The preservatives in treated wood are toxic to aquatic life. If you use treated wood, keep it from touching the water. If your bridge weathers over the years and you want to re-treat it, use a low-toxicity preservative and do not let any drip into the pond.

Use rustproof decking screws because nails may work their way loose. Drill pilot holes so the wood doesn't split.

Handrails offer a sense of security. If you build a handrail, be sure it will hold the weight of someone leaning against it. A rope railing is a simple alternative. Check building codes in your locale for requirements.

▲ **Add a sturdy handrail so that garden visitors can safely pause to enjoy the view.**

BENCH SEAT

A fter you have constructed, stocked, and landscaped a water garden, you will no doubt find your delightful oasis irresistible. The soothing music from a water feature cannot be ignored no matter what else is on your schedule. Design seating close to the pond so you can comfortably enjoy its sounds, sights, and activity.

Seating can be easy to design and build. A simple, rustic design may fit better in an informal setting around your pond than more contemporary patio furniture with fabric-covered cushion seats. You can piece together a bench seat from lumber scraps and found items or construct one from inexpensive materials purchased at a home-improvement store. When you build a bench, design the seat level at 16 to 20 inches high for the greatest comfort.

Even a big log placed lengthwise near the water's edge can be an inviting spot to sit in a naturalized aquascape. Peel the bark off so it won't snag clothing and insects won't have a hiding place.

If a 6- or 8-foot length of tree trunk is unavailable or too difficult to move, consider cutting shorter pieces to create stools. Stump stools are more easily relocated and can be charming and comfortable. You can group them together in conversation clusters or position one near each of the pond's best viewing points. A pair of stump stools can easily be made into a bench with the addition of a 2×12 plank or stone slab resting atop them.

In fact, a 2×12 plank of treated or untreated wood makes a simple bench seat that can be placed on top of easy-to-build legs. Today's treated, arsenic-free wood will last outdoors with a coat of paint or weatherproof finish or stain. You'll have to repaint or re-treat the seat annually to give it long-term protection from the elements. However, an untreated bench seat will weather naturally and help a newly built water garden design look mature.

If you don't have access to large tree trunks but can obtain sturdy 4- or 5-inch diameter tree branches, cut four of them to 18 inches and attach them to the plank with rustproof screws or nails.

Inexpensive 5-inch-round fence posts make simple bench legs. Fence posts are treated with preservatives and last a long time without any care. Cutting them to

▲ **Create a simple seat near the water's edge with wooden planks set atop concrete legs.**

▶ **Place your bench close enough to the pond that you can hear the water and watch the fish.**

BENCH SEAT *(continued)*

▲ A 1×10 plank attached to sturdy legs makes a simple bench. Add facing boards for stability and a finished look.

dozen leftover bricks or a pile of softball-size rocks. You'll want to build them in place because they will be too heavy to move when finished. Use a level to make sure your pillars are the same height and sitting square.

Thicker lumber seating made from a pair of 4×6 timbers will add enough height to the bench that the brick or stone pillars don't have to be as tall. Connect the timbers to each other with a couple of 1×2 lumber cross braces on the underside. You can embed a couple of protruding screws in the underside of the timbers right into the wet mortar.

length will be your biggest challenge. Because most power saws won't easily cut through 5-inch posts, you'll probably need to finish the cut with a handsaw.

Two-by-four lumber is easier to cut. You can make simple bench legs from four 20-inch lengths of 2×4 crossed in the center. Use a miter box to cut the ends at a 60° angle. Drill a ¼-inch hole in the center of each leg for a sturdy 5-inch bolt. Screw them to the 2×12 plank with 8 rustproof screws. For stability, attach a 2×4 brace from the center of one cross to the other with screws.

Two pairs of stacked cinder blocks make quick bench legs. Poke a couple of strong dowel rods into the ground on the inside of the stacked blocks so they don't slip apart and tip over. Use construction adhesive to glue the plank seat on top. Plant ivy at the base of each set to soften the look of harsh concrete, or paint the cinder blocks with a coat of bright paint to match the blooms on a nearby plant.

You can construct a pair of pillar bench legs with a bag of mortar and a couple of

▲ Seating made from tree trunks fits well with informal garden designs.

► A bench at the water's edge provides a relaxing spot to sit and watch the fish.

WATER GARDEN RESOURCES

You can find a variety of equipment, installation and maintenance supplies, ornaments, plants, and fish at water garden centers and nurseries. The following suppliers sell by mail order and through the Internet. Some offer colorful free catalogs with detailed information.

These resources are listed for your information only; no endorsement is implied or intended. Look in your phone directory for more water garden suppliers in your locale. Other pondkeepers can provide you with advice on building water features in your area.

Alita Industries
www.alita.com
626/962-2116
Pumps, lighting

Aqua Mart, Inc.
www.aqua-mart.com
800/245-5814
Ponds, waterfalls, fountains, plants

Aquatic Eco-Systems, Inc.
www.aquaticeco.com
877/347-4788
Maintenance tools, supplies

Creative Pondscapes
www.creativepondscapes.com
314/862-1400
Preformed and self-contained falls, streams, cover rocks

Gardenbridges.com
www.gardenbridges.com
866/690-9273
Ready-to-assemble and install wooden bridges

Green & Hagstrom
www.greenandhagstrom.com
615/799-0708
Aquatic nursery, water garden supplies

Hozelock Cyprio
www.hozelock.com
800/297-7461
Pond and waterfall pumps, filters, clarifiers

Lily Blooms
www.lilyblooms.com
800/921-0005
Plants, koi, liners, pumps, filters

Lilypons Water Gardens
www.lilypons.com
800/999-LILY
Supplies, equipment, pond kits, plants, fish

Natural Solutions
www.naturalsolutionsetc.com
315/531-8803
Natural products for pond management

OASE
www.oase-usa.com
Pumps, filters, lights, maintenance products

Paradise Water Gardens Ltd.
www.paradisewatergardens.com
800/955-0161
Supplies, equipment, plants, koi

The Pond Guy
www.thepondguy.com
888/766-3520
Pond kits, aquatic plants

Pondmakers.com
www.pondmakers.com
610/845-0380
Pumps, filters, liners

PondMart
www.pondmart.com
877/844-POND
Liners, pumps, filters, plants, lighting

Pond Supplier Co.
www.pondsupplier.com
888/692-7124
Waterfalls, pumps, skimmers, filters

Sacramento Koi
www.sacramentokoi.com
Designs, equipment for koi ponds

Still Pond Farm
www.stillpondfarm.com
800/527-9429
Natural products for pond management

The Water Garden
www.watergarden.com
423/870-2838
Waterfalls, bridges, lighting, plumbing

Van Ness Water Gardens
www.vnwg.com
800/205-2425
Equipment, plants

INDEX

Page numbers in *italic type* indicate photographs and illustrations.

METRIC CONVERSIONS

U.S. Units to Metric Equivalents			Metric Units to U.S. Equivalents		
To Convert From	Multiply By	To Get	To Convert From	Multiply By	To Get
Inches	25.4	Millimeters	Millimeters	0.0394	Inches
Inches	2.54	Centimeters	Centimeters	0.3937	Inches
Feet	30.48	Centimeters	Centimeters	0.0328	Feet
Feet	0.3048	Meters	Meters	3.2808	Feet
Yards	0.9144	Meters	Meters	1.0936	Yards
Square inches	6.4516	Square centimeters	Square centimeters	0.1550	Square inches
Square feet	0.0929	Square meters	Square meters	10.764	Square feet
Square yards	0.8361	Square meters	Square meters	1.1960	Square yards
Acres	0.4047	Hectares	Hectares	2.4711	Acres
Cubic inches	16.387	Cubic centimeters	Cubic centimeters	0.0610	Cubic inches
Cubic feet	0.0283	Cubic meters	Cubic meters	35.315	Cubic feet
Cubic feet	28.316	Liters	Liters	0.0353	Cubic feet
Cubic yards	0.7646	Cubic meters	Cubic meters	1.308	Cubic yards
Cubic yards	764.55	Liters	Liters	0.0013	Cubic yards

To convert from degrees Fahrenheit (F) to degrees Celsius (C), first subtract 32, then multiply by $\frac{5}{9}$.

To convert from degrees Celsius to degrees Fahrenheit, multiply by $\frac{9}{5}$, then add 32.

USDA PLANT HARDINESS ZONE MAP

This map of climate zones helps you select plants for your garden that will survive a typical winter in your region. The United States Department of Agriculture (USDA) developed the map, basing the zones on the lowest recorded temperatures across North America. Zone 1 is the coldest area and Zone 11 is the warmest.

Plants are classified by the coldest temperature and zone they can endure. For example, plants hardy to Zone 6 survive where winter temperatures drop to –10° F. Those hardy to Zone 8 die long before it's that cold. These plants may grow in colder regions but must be replaced each year. Plants rated for a range of hardiness zones can usually survive winter in the coldest region as well as tolerate the summer heat of the warmest one.

To find your hardiness zone, note the approximate location of your community on the map, then match the color band marking that area to the key.

HAWAII

AUSTRALIA

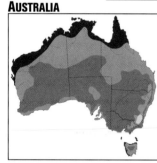

UNITED KINGDOM

Range of Average Annual Minimum Temperatures for Each Zone

Zone 1: Below -50° F (below -45.6° C)
Zone 2: -50 to -40° F (-45.5 to -40° C)
Zone 3: -40 to -30° F (-39.9 to -34.5° C)
Zone 4: -30 to -20° F (-34.4 to -28.9° C)
Zone 5: -20 to -10° F (-28.8 to -23.4° C)
Zone 6: -10 to 0° F (-23.3 to -17.8° C)
Zone 7: 0 to 10° F (-17.7 to -12.3° C)
Zone 8: 10 to 20° F (-12.2 to -6.7° C)
Zone 9: 20 to 30° F (-6.6 to -1.2° C)
Zone 10: 30 to 40° F (-1.1 to 4.4° C)
Zone 11: Above 40° F (above 4.5° C)

AVERAGE FROST DATES

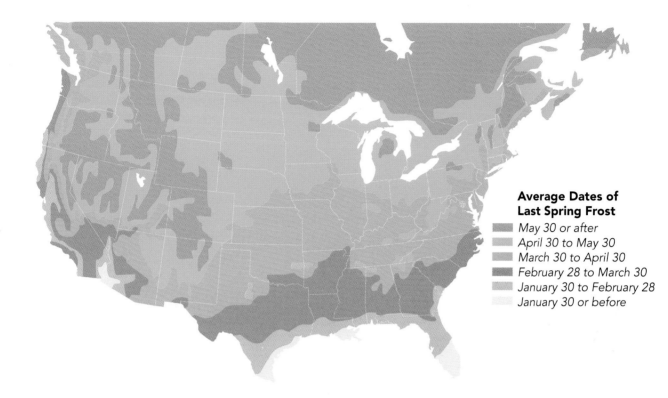

**Average Dates of
Last Spring Frost**

May 30 or after
April 30 to May 30
March 30 to April 30
February 28 to March 30
January 30 to February 28
January 30 or before

**Average Dates of
First Autumn Frost**

June 30 to July 30
July 30 to August 30
August 30 to September 30
September 30 to October 30
October 30 to November 30
November 30 to December 30

ORTHO ®

Better Homes and Gardens ®

watergardens

tranquility+beauty

Better Homes and Gardens.

WATER GARDENS
POOLS, STREAMS & FOUNTAINS

ORTHO

Creating
Water Gardens

BUILDING ▪ GROWING ▪ HOW-TO

ORTHO ALL ABOUT

Garden Pools
& Fountains
ALL NEW EDITION

expertadvice

inspiration+ideas+how-to
for designing, building, maintaining